The Essential Java™ Class Reference for Programmers

Third Edition

Brian Durney

PEARSON
Prentice
Hall

Upper Saddle River, NJ 07458

Library of Congress Cataloging in Publication Data

CIP Data on File

Vice President and Editorial Director, ECS: *Marcia J. Horton*
Publisher: *Alan R. Apt*
Associate Editor: *Toni Dianne Holm*
Editorial Assistant: *Patrick Lindner*
Vice President and Director of Production and Manufacturing, ESM: *David W. Riccardi*
Executive Managing Editor: *Vince O'Brien*
Managing Editor: *Camille Trentacoste*
Production Editor: *Lakshmi Balasubramanian*
Director of Creative Services: *Paul Belfanti*
Creative Director: *Carole Anson*
Art Director and Cover Manager: *Jayne Conte*
Managing Editor, AV Management and Production: *Patricia Burns*
Art Editor: *Gregory Dulles*
Manufacturing Manager: *Trudy Pisciotti*
Manufacturing Buyer: *Ilene Kahn*
Marketing Manager: *Pamela Shaffer*

© 2004 Pearson Education, Inc.
Pearson Prentice Hall
Pearson Education, Inc.
Upper Saddle River, NJ 07458

The author and publisher of this book have used their best efforts in preparing this book. These efforts include the development, research, and testing of the theories and programs to determine their effectiveness. The author and publisher make no warranty of any kind, expressed or implied, with regard to these programs or the documentation contained in this book. The author and publisher shall not be liable in any event for incidental or consequential damages in connection with, or arising out of, the furnishing, performance, or use of these programs.

Printed in the United States of America

10 9 8 7 6 5 4 3 2 1

ISBN 0-13-185645-6

Pearson Education Ltd., *London*
Pearson Education Australia Pty. Ltd., *Sydney*
Pearson Education Singapore, Pte. Ltd.
Pearson Education North Asia Ltd., *Hong Kong*
Pearson Education Canada, Inc., *Toronto*
Pearson Educación de Mexico, S.A. de C.V.
Pearson Education—Japan, *Tokyo*
Pearson Education Malaysia, Pte. Ltd.
Pearson Education, Inc., *Upper Saddle River, New Jersey*

The Essential Java™ Class Reference for Programmers

Third Edition

Table of Contents

Preface

This manual has been written to meet the demand for an easy-to-use guide to the rich resources available from Sun Microsystems to support the Java programming language.

The programming tools presented in this manual are very powerful, but often are not easily accessible to beginning programmers. In addition, descriptions of how to use these tools cannot easily be integrated into introductory textbooks. The manual is a perfect supplement to programming textbooks that focus on the Java language and its features. Here the focus is a hands-on and tutorial-style introduction to programming tools and resources.

Let's now look at the tools and resources covered in this manual.

One of the great features of the Java programming language is that it is available for free. You can download the Java Software Development Kit (SDK) from:

`http://java.sun.com`

Another great feature of Java is the Java API, which is a large library of classes that you can use in your programs. The classes in the API are useful because they make lots of things easier, including graphics and network communication, but there are many classes, with many methods, that can be confusing to beginning and intermediate Java programmers. The **Java Class Reference** section of this manual will help you find your way around the Java API. In the class reference, you'll find descriptions of the most commonly used classes and methods. In fact, the classes and methods presented were chosen by Prentice Hall textbook authors specifically because they will be the most useful for the beginning and intermediate Java programmer.

Even the best description can leave you wondering how to use a method in your program, so the class reference includes plenty of code examples, ranging from a single line of code to 10 or 20 lines. If you want to write a Java program and don't know where to start, turn to the **Complete Examples** chapter of the book. This chapter includes examples of both applications and applets. There is a GUI (Graphic User Interface) application and a text-interface application, so whatever kind of Java program you're writing, you'll find a starting point in this section.

If you like to show off your programs, you can put them on a Web site. Anyone in the world who has an Internet connection and a Java-enabled browser can try out your programs. Of course, a great applet deserves a great Web page, and the **HTML Tutorial** section will teach you how to put a Web page together and add your applet.

If you're new to programming, you've probably encountered a lot of unfamiliar terms or familiar terms used in unfamiliar ways. The **Java Programming Glossary** can help you figure out just what people are talking about when they mention "objects," "references," or any number of things related to Java programming. If you have some programming experience, but are new to Java, the glossary will help you learn terms that you might not be familiar with, like "exception" or "final."

Unfortunately, compilers are notorious for giving error messages that make no sense. Eventually you'll figure them all out, but until then you'll want to turn to the **Java Error Messages with Explanations** section of the book. There you'll find descriptions of errors that are more than one line long, as well as likely causes of the error.

ACKNOWLEDGMENTS

This reference manual wouldn't be possible without the Java language and documentation produced by Sun Microsystems. Sun's API description is the definitive documentation for Java classes and so was an important source of information for the **Java Class Reference** section.

I would like to thank everyone who contributed to this manual, including textbook authors and reviewers. Several people contributed to the list of classes to be included, and I appreciate their help in the difficult job of deciding which classes to include.

I also appreciate the help of the people at Prentice Hall who made this project possible and contributed in many ways.

Finally, I want to thank my great family: my wife, Kristy, and our children, Jessica, Alex, Jason, and Daniel. Nothing I do would be as good if they weren't part of my life.

C H A P T E R   1

Java Class Reference

As you design and write Java programs, there will be many opportunities to use classes from the Java API in your programs. Using API classes can save you time by allowing you to reuse a class instead of writing a new one. Using API classes can also improve the quality of your programs because the API classes have been more thoroughly tested than any code used by only one programmer. To realize the benefits of the Java API, it is important to be familiar with the API documentation and know how to find the information you need about the packages and classes it contains.

USING THE WEB-BASED API DOCUMENTATION

You can find documentation for the Java API on the Web at the address:

> http://java.sun.com/docs/index.html

When you go to that Web page, you have a choice of version, and you have the choice of downloading the documentation or browsing it on the Internet. Make your choice for the version of the Java API you are using, and choose between downloading and browsing, and then open the index page in your browser.

If you use the frame version of the documentation, you will see three frames in your browser window: a small frame in the upper-left corner, a vertical frame below it, and a larges frame on the right.

Use the upper-left frame to select a package to view. Your selection determines what classes will show up in the lower-left frame. If you choose **All Classes**, then it will display all the classes in the frame below, regardless of their package. If you choose a specific package, like `java.awt`, you will see only the classes (and interfaces) from that package in the frame below. Some packages, like `java.awt`, are large and contain many classes. Other packages, like `java.applet`, are small.

When you click on a class in the lower-left frame, you will see documentation for the class displayed in the main window. That documentation includes the class's place in the inheritance hierarchy, an overview description of the class, and summaries and descriptions of the inner classes, constructors, fields (constants and variables), and methods of the class.

Besides selecting a class by using the frames on the left, you have several other options for browsing the API documentation. At the top of the main (largest) frame, there are several links, including **Tree** and **Index**.

If you click on the **Tree** link, you will see classes in hierarchical format, with classes farther down in the hierarchy appearing farther to the left, and with each class appearing somewhere below its parent. The name of each class is a link which you can click on to see the documentation for that class. Note that going to the class description in this way does not change the frames on the left.

If you click on the **Index** link, you can browse the documentation in alphabetical order. Every letter of the alphabet has a link at the top of the page, and if you click on a letter you can scroll through all the classes, constructors, methods, and fields that begin with that letter. Each member (constructor, method, or field) of a class has a link to its documentation, as well as a link to its class's documentation.

DOCUMENTATION FOR SELECTED PACKAGES AND CLASSES

The API documentation available on the Web is complete and is an important resource. However, there will be times when your screen is already full of windows, or you don't have access to the Internet or a computer, or you just don't want to bother looking through *every* method in a class. That's where the documentation in this section comes in. You can carry it with you anywhere, write notes in the margins, and do all of the things you can do with a book, without taking up screen space. Also, the classes and methods in this section have been selected because they are commonly used, so you don't have to search through the more obscure methods and classes in the Java API.

The packages in this section are listed in alphabetic order, with classes in alphabetic order within each package. Selected methods of the class are in related groups (for instance, set- and get-methods for a given property are together) or alphabetical. Some descriptions include references to the **Complete Examples** section, which follows this section.

The java.util package includes a set of classes and interfaces used for working with collections in Java (such as lists, sets, and vectors). The java.util section is divided into two sections so that all the collection classes and interfaces are in the same section.

In some cases, a text description of a method is not necessary because the method name and parameter types (and descriptive names) are sufficient. In other cases, space doesn't allow a full description, but the method name and parameters are a useful reminder if you don't remember the exact name or order of the parameters. In these cases, only the method name and parameters are listed.

Note that all the methods and constants listed here are `public`, unless otherwise declared. All constructors are `public`, and constructors never have a return type.

java.applet Package

This is a small package that includes just one class (and several interfaces, two of which are described here).

Applet Class

Every Java applet will use the `Applet` class, but most or all of them will use it indirectly. The usual way to use `Applet` is to make a new class that extends it rather than create objects of the `Applet` class directly.

An applet class inherits from `Component` and from `Container`. As a descendant of `Container`, it can have other components added to it, and uses a layout manager to arrange them.

The Swing package contains `JApplet`, a newer class that can be used for applets in Web pages. Even applets that extend the `JApplet` class are indirectly using the `Applet` class, because `JApplet` inherits from `Applet`.

An applet class contains two kinds of methods—those that override methods in the parent class, and those that are called from the child class. In the first category, methods that are often overridden, are `init`, `start`, `paint`, `stop`, and `destroy`. Of these five methods, the most commonly used are `init` and `paint`. Note that `paint` is inherited from `Component`, not `Applet`.

Methods

- `void init()`
This method is called by the browser or appletviewer after the applet is loaded.

- `void start()`
This method is called by the browser or appletviewer when the applet is ready to start execution.

- `void paint(Graphics)`
This method is inherited from **Component**. It is called whenever the applet needs to be redrawn on the screen. Applets that use graphics, like drawing shapes or bitmaps on the screen, usually do so in this method.

- `void stop()`
This method is called after the applet is stopped.

- `void destroy()`
This method is called when the applet has finished execution.

In addition to the methods listed above, which an applet class often overrides, there are many useful methods in the parent class of **Applet**. Some of the more common ones are:

- `String getParameter(String name)`
This method returns the value of a parameter. Parameters are information that can be passed to an applet from the HTML document. In that way, the applet can be adapted to various situations without having to change code or recompile.

- `URL getDocumentBase()`
- `URL getCodeBase()`
Often it is useful for an applet to read files or obtain media resources. For security reasons, an applet is not allowed to access arbitrary files. However, an applet

can always load files from the same directory that contains its document (an HTML file). The URL for that directory is returned by the method **getDocu-mentBase()**. Similarly, an applet can load files from the directory that contains its class file. The directory can be accessed using the URL returned by the method **getCodeBase()**.

Two similar methods are **getImage** and **getAudioClip**. Each has two versions, one that takes a single parameter, and another that takes two parameters. The two-parameter versions concatenate the name parameter with the **url** parameter.

- **Image getImage(URL url)**
- **Image getImage(URL url, String name)**

This method gets an image, but the image will not actually be loaded until it is drawn. The **SpotlightApplet** example uses the two-parameter **getImage** method.
    For the two-parameter methods, the methods **getDocumentBase** and **get-CodeBase** are often used. For instance, the following line of code would get the image file myPic.jpg from the directory that contains the applet's HTML file:

```
Image myImage = getImage(getDocumentBase(), "myPic.jpg");
```

- **AudioClip getAudioClip(URL url)**
- **AudioClip getAudioClip(URL url, String name)**

This method is used to get an audio clip, but the clip will not actually be loaded until its **play** method is called.
Here is an example of using **getAudioClip**:

```
AudioClip sound;
try {
    URL soundURL = new URL(getDocumentBase(), "mysound.au");
    sound = getAudioClip(soundURL);
    sound.play();
}
catch (Exception ex) {
    System.out.println(ex);
}
```

This example shows a sound file in **.au** format. More recent versions of Java allow **.wav** and AIFF format sounds, but older Web browsers use an older version of Java and might not support these sound formats.

- **public AppletContext getAppletContext()**

This method returns an object that implements the interface **AppletContext**. The context could be a browser or the appletviewer. The context object provides several methods, including **getApplet** and **showDocument**.

AppletContext Interface

AppletContext is an interface, not a class. An object that implements this interface will usually be a Web browser or an appletviewer. This interface includes the methods **getApplet** and **showDocument**.

Methods

- **void showDocument(URL url)**
- **void showDocument(URL url, String target)**

The URL passed as a parameter will be displayed as the current page. Note that applet contexts of some kinds, such as an appletviewer, might ignore this method.

The two-parameter version allows the caller to specify which window should show the document. Options for the target include **"_self"** to replace the page that contains the applet, **"_blank"** to show the document in a new browser window, and a window name to show the document in a specified window. See the **ShowDocApplet** example for a sample use of this method.

- **Applet getApplet(String name)**

This method returns a reference to another applet on the same HTML page. Using this method, one complicated applet can be split into several simpler applets that communicate to do the same job. That way, the program is more modular, and each of the applets can be replaced or modified independently, provided that the new applet provides the same interface.

AudioClip Interface

AudioClip is an interface that allows a program to play sounds. More than one sound can be playing at the same time. Java 2 programs can play sounds in **.au** format and **.wav** format, but earlier versions of Java can only play **.au** files.

Methods

- **void loop()**

This method repeatedly plays the sound.

- **void play()**

This method plays the sound.

- **void stop()**

This method stops the sound from playing.

java.awt Package

AWT stands for "Abstract Window Toolkit." This package includes many classes used for working with windows (of course) and other GUI components, such as buttons, menus, and text areas. It also includes classes and subpackages used for working with graphics and images.

BorderLayout Class

The **BorderLayout** class divides a container into five regions: **North**, **South**, **East**, **West**, and **Center**. When the container grows, the **Center** region gets taller and wider. The **North** and **South** regions get wider but not taller, and the **East** and **West** regions get taller but not wider.

Constants

- **static final String NORTH**
- **static final String SOUTH**
- **static final String EAST**
- **static final String WEST**
- **static final String CENTER**

These constants are used to specify where a component should be added to the container.

Constructors

- **BorderLayout()**
- **BorderLayout(int hgap, int vgap)**

The second constructor specifies the horizontal and vertical gaps between components.

Methods

- **int getHgap()**
- **void setHgap(int hgap)**
- **int getVgap()**
- **void setVgap(int vgap)**

These methods get and set the horizontal or vertical gaps between components.

Button Class

Constructors

- **Button()**
- **Button(String label)**

Methods

- **String getLabel()**
- **void setLabel(String label)**

The label of a button is the text that will show on the face of the button.

- **void setActionCommand(String command)**
- **String getActionCommand()**

The action command provides a way to tell which button the user has clicked. An action event object contains the action command for the clicked button, which can be matched with the string returned by the **getActionCommand** method in the **Button** class. If no action command is specified, use the **setActionCommand** method; the action command will be the button's label.

- **void addActionListener(ActionListener l)**
- **void removeActionListener(ActionListener l)**
- **EventListener[] getListeners(Class listenerType)**

An action listener class will contain the **actionPerformed** method, which will be called when the button is clicked.

CardLayout Class

The **CardLayout** manager is useful for switching back and forth between several "cards." Each card is a component that has been added to the container managed by the **CardLayout** object. A card can be a simple component, like a button or a text area, or it can be a panel, which is a container. Each card takes up the container's entire space on the screen while it is being displayed.

Constructors

- **CardLayout()**
- **CardLayout(int hgap, int vgap)**

The first constructor, with no parameters, sets the vertical and horizontal gaps between components to zero. The second constructor has parameters used to set the gaps between components.

Methods

- **void first(Container parent)**
- **void last(Container parent)**
- **void next(Container parent)**
- **void previous(Container parent)**

These methods are all used to change the display from one card to another. The card sequence is determined by the order in which they are added to the container.

- **void show(Container parent, String name)**

Displays the card named by the second parameter. Cards are given names when they are added to the parent container.

Checkbox Class

The **Checkbox** class is a component that the user can switch on or off. A check box has a label that is usually used to tell the user what the check box means. The state of the check box indicates whether the user has turned it on (**true**) or off (**false**). In a group of check boxes, if one check box is turned on, the others will be turned off. Check boxes in a group are different in appearance from check boxes that are not part of a group.

Constructors

- **Checkbox()**
- **Checkbox(String label)**
- **Checkbox(String label, boolean state)**
- **Checkbox(String label, CheckboxGroup group, boolean state)**

Parameters to the constructors can specify the label, the state, and the group for the check box.

Methods

- **String getLabel()**
- **void setLabel(String label)**

These methods get and set the check box label.

- **`boolean getState()`**
- **`void setState(boolean state)`**

These methods get and set the check box state.

- **`CheckboxGroup getCheckboxGroup()`**
- **`void setCheckboxGroup(CheckboxGroup g)`**

These methods get and set the check box group.

- **`void addItemListener(ItemListener l)`**

This method adds a listener for the check box. The listener will receive an event when the user changes the state of the check box.

CheckboxGroup Class

A group of check boxes is used to show the user a set of mutually exclusive options. If one check box is selected, all the others in the group will be deselected. To make a group of check boxes, you can make the group and pass it as a parameter in the constructor for each check box, or you can use the **`setCheckboxGroup`** method of the **`Checkbox`** class.

Constructors

- **`CheckboxGroup()`**

Methods

- **`Checkbox getSelectedCheckbox()`**

This method returns a reference to the check box that has been selected. Only one check box in a group may be selected at one time.

- **`void setSelectedCheckbox(Checkbox box)`**

This method sets the state of the parameter to **`true`** and sets the state of all the other check boxes in the group to **`false`**. You can set the state of all the check boxes to **`false`** by passing in a null parameter.

Color Class

The **`Color`** class is used to define colors in Java, including background colors and text colors. The class includes constants for various colors:

Constants

- **`static Color black`**
- **`static Color blue`**
- **`static Color cyan`**
- **`static Color darkGray`**
- **`static Color gray`**
- **`static Color green`**
- **`static Color lightGray`**
- **`static Color magenta`**
- **`static Color orange`**
- **`static Color pink`**
- **`static Color red`**
- **`static Color white`**
- **`static Color yellow`**

Constructors

- `Color(int r, int g, int b)`
- `Color(float r, float g, float b)`

The three parameters for these constructors tell how much red, green, and blue will be in the color represented by the new object. The `SpotlightApplet` example includes the following line, which is used to set the background color of the applet:

```
setBackground(new Color(20, 2, 60));
```

The constructor used in this case is the one that takes **int** parameters. The color produced contains some blue (third argument) and a little red (first argument), but not much green at all (second argument). The maximum value for integer parameters is 255, and the minimum is 0. If all three parameters are 255, the color will be white, and if all three are 0, the color will be black. Colors with lower values are generally darker than colors with higher values.

The constructor that takes **float** parameters works in a similar way, except that instead of using a range from 0 to 255, the **float** parameters should be in the range 0.0–1.0.

Methods

- `static Color decode(String numStr) throws NumberFormatException`

This method can be used to specify a hexadecimal value for a color. The first two hex digits specify the blue component, the second two specify the green component, and the last two specify the red component.

The following code can be used in an applet to get an applet parameter called **TextColor** and then convert the string parameter to a **Color** object that can be used in the applet:

```
textColor = Color.decode(getParameter("TextColor"));
```

The applet parameter can be set in the HTML for the applet by using tags like this one:

```
<APPLET CODE=CharDisplayApplet HEIGHT=125 WIDTH=250>
<PARAM NAME=TextColor VALUE=0xFFFF99>
</APPLET>
```

- `Color darker()`
- `Color brighter()`

These two methods can be used to adjust the brightness of a color, as described by the name of the method. These can be used with the color constants in the **Color** class, as follows:

```
Color darkBlue = Color.blue.darker();
```

Since the **darker()** method returns a **Color** object, you could use a one like this one to make an even darker shade of blue:

```
Color darkBlue = Color.blue.darker().darker();
```

Component Class

The **Component** class is an ancestor of many AWT classes, including **Container** and its descendants (**Frame**, **Panel**, **Applet**) and also including **Button**, **Canvas**, **Checkbox**,

`Choice`, `Container`, `Label`, `List`, `Scrollbar`, `TextArea`, and `TextField`. Since `JComponent` inherits from `Container`, which inherits from `Component`, `Swing` components also inherit from `Component`.

Some of the many methods of `Component` are listed below. These methods are normally used in classes that inherit them from `Component`.

Methods

- `String getName()`
- `void setName(String name)`
- `Container getParent()`
- `boolean isVisible()`
- `boolean isShowing()`
- `boolean isEnabled()`
- `void setEnabled(boolean b)`

If a component is disabled, it will be dimmed and the user will not be able to click on it or otherwise use it.

- `void setVisible(boolean b)`
- `Color getForeground()`
- `void setForeground(Color c)`

The foreground color is the color used for text in the component.

- `Color getBackground()`
- `void setBackground(Color c)`
- `Font getFont()`
- `void setFont(Font f)`
- `Point getLocation()`
- `Point getLocationOnScreen()`
- `void setLocation(int x, int y)`
- `void setLocation(Point p)`
- `Dimension getSize()`
- `void setSize(int width, int height)`
- `void setSize(Dimension d)`
- `Rectangle getBounds()`
- `void setBounds(int x, int y, int width, int height)`
- `void setBounds(Rectangle r)`
- `int getX()`
- `int getY()`
- `int getWidth()`
- `int getHeight()`
- `Rectangle getBounds(Rectangle rv)`

- `Dimension getSize(Dimension rv)`
- `Point getLocation(Point rv)`
- `Dimension getPreferredSize()`
- `Dimension getMinimumSize()`
- `Dimension getMaximumSize()`
- `Graphics getGraphics()`
- `void setCursor(Cursor cursor)`
- `Cursor getCursor()`
- `void paint(Graphics g)`

For components like canvases, applets, frames, and panels, this method can be overridden to draw on the component using methods from the **Graphics** class.

- `void update(Graphics g)`

This method updates a component by filling it in with the background color, setting the color of the graphics context to the foreground color, and then calling the paint method to redraw the component.

- `void repaint()`
- `void repaint(int x, int y, int width, int height)`

The **repaint** method causes a component to be updated. The **update** method will be called, which in turn will call the **paint** method for the component (unless the **update** method has been overridden).

- `boolean contains(int x, int y)`
- `boolean contains(Point p)`
- `Component getComponentAt(int x, int y)`
- `Component getComponentAt(Point p)`
- `void addKeyListener(KeyListener l)`
- `void removeKeyListener(KeyListener l)`
- `void addMouseListener(MouseListener l)`
- `void removeMouseListener(MouseListener l)`
- `void addMouseMotionListener(MouseMotionListener l)`
- `void removeMouseMotionListener(MouseMotionListener l)`
- `EventListener[] getListeners(Class listenerType)`

These methods are used to add and remove listeners for various kinds of events. The methods listed here are for some of the more commonly used listeners. There are other listeners that can be used with components, including component listeners, focus listeners, and hierarchy bounds listeners.

- `void requestFocus()`
- `void transferFocus()`
- `boolean hasFocus()`
- `void add(PopupMenu popup)`
- `void remove(MenuComponent popup)`

Container Class

A container is a component to which other components may be added. Every container class has a layout manager that arranges the components within it.

Methods

- **public Component add(Component comp)**
- **Component add(Component comp, int index)**
- **void remove(int index)**
- **void remove(Component comp)**
- **void removeAll()**
- **LayoutManager getLayout()**
- **void setLayout(LayoutManager mgr)**

The layout managers that can be added to a container include **BorderLayout**, **BoxLayout**, **CardLayout**, **FlowLayout**, **GridLayout**, and **GridBagLayout**.

- **int getComponentCount()**
- **Component getComponent(int n)**
- **Component[] getComponents()**
- **Insets getInsets()**
- **void invalidate()**
- **void validate()**

This method validates the layout of the component. When the components added to a container component have been changed, the program should call this method to make sure that the layout is correctly done. Calling the validate method is especially important after components have been removed.

- **void paintComponents(Graphics g)**

Dialog Class

A **Dialog** is a window that is associated with another window. The dialog window's owner can be a frame or another dialog. Dialog windows are generally used to get input from the user. If the dialog is modal, then the user cannot use any other window for the same program until the dialog is closed. By default, a dialog window is not modal.

Methods

- **Dialog(Dialog owner)**
- **Dialog(Dialog owner, String title)**
- **Dialog(Dialog owner, String title, boolean modal)**
- **Dialog(Frame owner)**
- **Dialog(Frame owner, boolean modal)**
- **Dialog(Frame owner, String title)**
- **Dialog(Frame owner, String title, boolean modal)**

- **void addNotify()**
- **boolean isModal()**
- **void setModal(boolean b)**
- **String getTitle()**
- **void setTitle(String title)**
- **void show()**

This method makes the dialog window appear on the screen.

- **void hide()**
- **void dispose()**

Resources that are allocated to show the dialog window will be released when the dispose method is called. The dialog is not displayable until **pack** or **show** is called.

- **boolean isResizable()**
- **void setResizable(boolean resizable)**

Dimension Class

The **Dimension** class is convenient for representing sizes. It includes height and width variables.

Variables

- **int width**
- **int height**

Constructors

- **Dimension()**
- **Dimension(Dimension d)**
- **Dimension(int width, int height)**

Methods

- **double getWidth()**
- **double getHeight()**
- **void setSize(double width, double height)**
- **void setSize(int width, int height)**
- **boolean equals(Object obj)**

Event Class

Java programs rarely create new events, so the constructors for the **Event** class are not often used and are not listed here. When a program receives an event, it is usually dealing with a more specific kind of event, like a **MouseEvent** or a **KeyEvent**.

Methods

- **boolean shiftDown()**
- **boolean controlDown()**
- **boolean metaDown()**

These methods are used to tell whether the Shift, Control, or Alt (Meta) key was pressed at the time the event occurred. Use of these methods allows the program to handle a Shift-click differently than a click.

FlowLayout Class

The flow layout is the simplest of the layout managers. It displays components from left to right in the order in which they were added to the container.

Constants

- **static final int CENTER**
- **static final int LEFT**
- **static final int RIGHT**

Used to specify the alignment of the rows of components in the container.

Constructors

- **FlowLayout()**
- **FlowLayout(int align)**
- **FlowLayout(int align, int hgap, int vgap)**

The **hgap** and **vgap** parameters specify the horizontal and vertical gaps between components. The alignment can be left, center, or right, specified by use of the constants listed above.

FileDialog Class

A file dialog is a specialized type of dialog window that allows a user to select a file to open, or select the file name and directory for saving a file. A **Swing** class called **JFile-Chooser** provides similar functionality.

The **PictureFrame** application in the **Complete Examples** section uses a **File-Dialog**, so you can refer to that example to see sample code.

Constants

- **static final int LOAD**
- **static final int SAVE**

The **LOAD** and **SAVE** constants are values used as the mode for the three-parameter constructor and the **getMode** and **setMode** methods. The file dialog will operate differently depending on whether the use is opening a file (**LOAD**) or saving a file (**SAVE**).

Constructors

- **FileDialog(Frame parent)**
- **FileDialog(Frame parent, String title)**

- `FileDialog(Frame parent, String title, int mode)`

The file dialog is hidden when the parent frame is hidden or minimized, and made visible again when the parent is made visible.

Methods

- `int getMode()`
- `void setMode(int mode)`
- `String getDirectory()`
- `String getFile()`

These two methods are used to find out the user's choice of file. To open the file, the directory should be concatenated with the file name to get the full path to the file.

- `void setDirectory(String dir)`
- `void setFile(String file)`
- `void show()`

This method is inherited from the **Window** class. To make the file dialog appear on the screen, call this method. Since file dialogs are modal, this method does not return until the user clicks selects a file to open or save, or clicks on Cancel.

Font Class

The **Font** class is used to set the font used in components, such as the label for a button or the text that appears in a text area. The availability of fonts is system-dependent, so the fonts available on one system might not be available on another.

Constants

- `static final int PLAIN`
- `static final int BOLD`
- `static final int ITALIC`

These constants are passed as parameters to a constructor to indicate the style of the font. They are also returned as values of the **getStyle** method.

Constructors

- `Font(String name, int style, int size)`

The name for a new font object is the name of a font family like "Helvetica." The style can be either **PLAIN**, **BOLD**, **ITALIC**, or **BOLD + ITALIC** (for both italic and bold). The size is in points, with bigger numbers representing bigger characters on the screen. The characters from one font will not always be the same size as characters in another font with the same point size.

Methods   The following methods are used to get information about a font:

- `String getFamily()`
- `String getFontName()`

- **int getSize()**
- **int getStyle()**
- **boolean isBold()**
- **boolean isItalic()**
- **boolean isPlain()**

The **getStyle** method returns the style of the font as an integer, so to find out what the style is you need to compare the return value to the constants for **PLAIN**, **BOLD**, **ITALIC**, and **BOLD + ITALIC**. The return values from **isBold**, **isItalic**, and **isPlain** are easier to interpret.

Here is sample code that shows how a constructor can be used to make a font object, and various methods can then be used to find the properties of the font:

```
Font myFont =
        new Font("Helvetica", Font.BOLD + Font.ITALIC, 24);
System.out.println("family: " + myFont.getFamily());
System.out.println("font name: " + myFont.getFontName());
System.out.println("size: " + myFont.getSize());
System.out.println("isPlain: " + myFont.isPlain());
System.out.println("isBold: " + myFont.isBold());
System.out.println("isItalic: " + myFont.isItalic());
```

The preceding lines of code gave the following output:

```
family: sansserif.bolditalic
font name: sansserif.bolditalic
size: 24
isPlain: false
isBold: true
isItalic: true
```

FontMetrics Class

In order to center text that is drawn on a canvas, your program needs information about how wide a string will be when displayed in a given font. The **FontMetrics** class provides that information, and also gives information about how high a text string will be.

Note that some of the metrics are defined for the font as a whole, and some are in terms of a particular string. Sizes are in pixels.

Constructors

- **protected FontMetrics(Font font)**

The parameter is the font for which the new object will give height and width information.

Methods

- **int stringWidth(String str)**

Gives the width of the string parameter when displayed with the font passed to the constructor. Other methods in the **FontMetrics** class provide information about the width of characters, but remember that the sum of the widths of the characters in a string is not necessarily the same as the width of a string of the same characters.

- **int getLeading()**

This method tells the amount of space between lines. The leading is the space between the descent of one line of text and the ascent of the line below it.

- **int getAscent()**
- **int getMaxAscent()**

This method tells the standard (**getAscent**) or maximum (**getMaxAscent**) distance from the baseline to the top of a character in the font.

- **int getDescent()**
- **int getMaxDescent()**

This method tells the standard (**getDescent**) or maximum (**getMaxDescent**) distance from the baseline to the bottom of a character in the font.

- **int getHeight()**

This method tells the height of a line of text. The height is the sum of the leading, the ascent, and the descent. The value returned is the standard height, not the maximum height; some characters may be taller and overlap with other lines.

Frame Class

The **Frame** class is commonly used to make a window for a GUI application. A frame will not appear on the screen until the **show** method (inherited from the **Window** class) is called. Since a frame can have a menu bar, the class includes methods to get, set, and remove menu bars. In order to make the close button on the frame work, the frame must have a **WindowListener**.

See the sample code at the end of this class description for an example of making a frame with a working close button. You can also refer to the **PictureFrame** example in the **Complete Examples** section to see an application that uses a **Frame**.

Constructors

- **Frame()**
- **Frame(String title)**

Methods

- **void setResizable(boolean resizable)**

If this method is called with the value **true**, the user will be able to change the size of the frame.

- **MenuBar getMenuBar()**
- **void setMenuBar(MenuBar mb)**

These methods get and set the menu bar for the frame.

- **void remove(MenuComponent m)**

This method removes a menu bar from the frame.

Example Here is sample code for showing a frame with a working close button. Note that all of the methods for the **WindowListener** interface must be defined, or the program will not compile. In this example, all but one of the methods do nothing. The **windowClosing** button calls **System.exit** to end the program.

```java
import java.awt.*;
import java.awt.event.*;

class FrameApp extends Frame implements WindowListener {
    public FrameApp () {
    addWindowListener(this);
    }

    public void windowOpened(WindowEvent e) {}
    public void windowClosing(WindowEvent e) {
      System.exit(0);
    }
    public void windowClosed(WindowEvent e) {}
    public void windowIconified(WindowEvent e) {}
    public void windowDeiconified(WindowEvent e) {}
    public void windowActivated(WindowEvent e) {}
    public void windowDeactivated(WindowEvent e) {}

    public static void main(String[] args) {
      FrameApp win = new FrameApp();
      win.setSize(300, 200);
      win.show();
    }
}
```

Graphics Class

The **Graphics** class provides methods for drawing on the screen. Some methods draw shapes, others draw bitmap images, and others set properties, including colors, fonts, and the clipping area.

Methods

- **void setColor(Color c)**
This method sets the color for the graphics object. The parameter to the method will be the color used by subsequent draw and fill methods for shapes, like **drawRect**. The same color will be used to draw text on the screen.

- **void drawRect(int x, int y, int width, int height)**
- **void drawOval(int x, int y, int width, int height)**
- **void fillRect(int x, int y, int width, int height)**
- **void fillOval(int x, int y, int width, int height)**
- **void drawRoundRect(int x, int y, int width, int height,**
                                      int arcWidth, int arcHeight)
- **boolean drawImage(Image img, int x, int y,**
                                      ImageObserver observer)

This method draws the image passed as the first parameter at a place specified by the x and y parameters.

The last parameter must either be **null** or a reference to an object that implements the **ImageObserver** interface. The image observer is important because the image cannot be drawn until it has been loaded. If an image observer is supplied, then the **drawImage** method will update the image when it has been loaded. If no observer is supplied, then the image will not be drawn if it has not already been loaded. The **Component** class implements the **ImageObserver** interface, so a reference to any **Component** object can be passed as the last parameter.

- **void setClip(int x, int y, int width, int height)**
- **void setClip(Shape clip)**

The clipping area of a graphics context determines what part of the graphics page can be changed by drawing commands. The first **setClip** method listed above can be used to set the clipping area to a rectangle specified by its upper-left corner and its dimensions. The second **setClip** method takes an arbitrary shape, which could be a polygon, an oval, a rectangle, or another kind of shape. Note that a **Shape** clip won't work with some earlier versions of Java.

A clipping area is useful for drawing just part of an image. There are two ways to use clipping areas to allow a program to show the user different parts of an image. By keeping the clipping area stationary and moving the image, your program can pan across an image. Or you can keep the image still and move the clipping area to show different parts of the image. This second option is used in the **SpotlightApplet** example (in the **Complete Examples** section).

GridBagConstraints Class

This class is used in conjunction with the **GridBagLayout** class. Each **GridBagConstraints** object has a number of variables that can be set. The constraints object, along with a component, is passed to the **setConstraints** method of the **GridBagLayout**, which uses the constraints to determine the position and size of the component.

Variables

- **int anchor**

This variable is used to tell where a component is placed within its display area. The direction constants (**EAST**, **WEST**, etc.) and **CENTER** can be used as values for this variable, with **CENTER** being the default.

- **int fill**

This variable is given a value of **BOTH**, **HORIZONTAL**, **VERTICAL**, or **NONE**, to indicate how the component should grow or shrink when the container changes size.

- **int gridheight**

This variable tells how many rows of the grid the component should span. It can be given an unnamed integer value or **REMAINDER** or **RELATIVE**. **REMAINDER** specifies that the component will be the last one in its column, and **RELATIVE** specifies that it will be next to last.

- **int gridwidth**

This variable tells how many columns of the grid the component should span. It can be given an unnamed integer value or **REMAINDER** or **RELATIVE**. **REMAINDER** specifies that the component will be the last one in its row and **RELATIVE** specifies that it will be next to last.

- **int gridx**

This variable specifies the column of the component in the grid. The value **RELATIVE** indicates that the component should be added just to the right of the preceding component.

- **int gridy**

This variable specifies the row of the component in the grid. The value **RELATIVE** indicates that the component should be added just below the preceding component.

- **Insets insets**

This variable tells how much space to leave between the component and the edges of its display area.

- **int ipadx**

This variable specifies the amount of space to add to the minimum width of the component.

- **int ipady**

This variable specifies the amount of space to add to the minimum width of the component.

- **double weightx**

This variable tells how much extra horizontal space should be allocated to the component, with zero indicating that no additional space should be given to it.

- **double weighty**

This variable tells how much extra vertical space should be allocated to the component, with zero indicating that no additional space should be given to it.

Constants

- **static int BOTH**
- **static int HORIZONTAL**
- **static int VERTICAL**
- **static int NONE**

The preceding four constants are used as values for the **fill** variable.

- **static int CENTER**
- **static int EAST**
- **static int NORTH**
- **static int NORTHEAST**
- **static int NORTHWEST**
- **static int SOUTH**
- **static int SOUTHEAST**
- **static int SOUTHWEST**
- **static int WEST**

The preceding named constants are used as values for the **anchor** variable.

- **static int RELATIVE**
- **static int REMAINDER**

The preceding two constants are used for values for the **gridheight**, **gridwidth**, **gridx**, and **gridy** variables.

Constructors

- **GridBagConstraints()**

All variables are set to their default values.

- **GridBagConstraints(int gridx, int gridy, int gridwidth,**
  int gridheight, double weightx, double weighty,
  int anchor, int fill, Insets insets, int ipadx,
  int ipady)

This constructor is used to specify all the variables in the new **Constraints** object. It is not often used. Instead, a **Constraints** object with default values is constructed, and then variables are set as desired.

GridBagLayout Class

The grid bag layout can be used for complicated layouts where components span the rows or columns of a grid, and where some components are weighted more heavily than others. Usually you will need to make at least one object of class **GridBagConstraints** and then use it to specify the constraints for each component.

Constructors

- **GridBagLayout()**

Usually you will need to keep a reference to the **GridBagLayout** object that you create with the constructor.

Methods

- **void setConstraints(Component comp,**
  GridBagConstraints constraints)

This method is called for each component that is added to the container, before the component is added to the container.

GridLayout Class

The grid layout arranges components in a grid of rows of columns. Components are added to the grid starting with the first column of the first row and filling all the columns in a row before adding any components to the next row. All the components in the grid are the same size, and they grow or shrink equally when the container grows or shrinks.

Constructors

- **GridLayout()**
- **GridLayout(int rows, int cols)**

- **GridLayout(int rows, int cols, int hgap, int vgap)**

As with all of the layout managers, parameters to the constructor can specify the vertical and horizontal gaps between components. The parameters can also specify the number of rows and columns in the grid of components.

Methods

- **void setColumns(int cols)**
- **void setRows(int rows)**

Image Class

The **Image** class provides a means for manipulating bitmap pictures.

- **abstract int getHeight(ImageObserver observer)**
- **abstract int getWidth(ImageObserver observer)**

These methods take an image observer as a parameter so that the height and width information can be updated later if the image has not been completely loaded when the method is called.

One use for this information is to center an image in a screen area. For instance, to center an image in an applet, a program can use code like this in a method in the **paint** method of an applet:

```
// myImage is declared and given a value elsewhere
Image myImage;

public void paint(Graphics page) {
    int x, y, height, width;
    height = myImage.getWidth(this);
    width = myImage.getHeight(this);
    x = (getWidth() - height) / 2;
    y = (getHeight() - width) / 2;
    page.drawImage(myImage, x, y, this);
}
```

Label Class

A label is a component used to display a single line of text which the user cannot edit. The text of a label can be changed by a program using methods available in the class. The colors and font of a label can be set using methods inherited from **Component**.

Constants

- **static final int LEFT**
- **static final int CENTER**
- **static final int RIGHT**

These three constants are used to specify alignment of text within a label.

Constructors

- **Label()**
- **Label(String text)**

- `Label(String text, int alignment)`

If no alignment is specified to the constructor, then the text will be aligned on the left.

Methods

- `int getAlignment()`
- `void setAlignment(int alignment)`
- `String getText()`
- `void setText(String text)`

MediaTracker Class

This class provides a way for a program to monitor the downloading process for images. By using this class, a program can avoid the problem of attempting to display an image before it has been downloaded. A program can also use information from this class to inform the user of progress in downloading images.

The basic idea of the `MediaTracker` class is that you can add images to the tracker and then check the status of the downloading or wait for all the pictures to finish downloading. By downloading a group of images at one time, and informing the user of the progress, you can avoid random delays while your program is running. For instance, if your program will be displaying an animation, it is better to download all of the images for the animation at once, so that the animation can run smoothly once it starts.

Constants

- `static final int LOADING`
- `static final int ABORTED`
- `static final int ERRORED`
- `static final int COMPLETE`

These constants are used to indicate the status of downloading images.

Methods

- `void addImage(Image image, int id)`

This method adds an image to the list of images tracked by a `MediaTracker` object. The ID is a number used to refer to the image later. The ID of images does not have to be unique, so you can track a group of images with one ID.

- `void addImage(Image image, int id, int w, int h)`

The second of the two `addImage` methods is used if you want to track an image that is being scaled. The `w` and `h` parameters are the width and height to which the image will be scaled.

The following methods check the status of loading images:
- `boolean checkAll()`

Returns true if all images have finished loading, have been aborted, or have an error.

- **boolean checkID(int id)**

Returns true if all images with the specified ID have finished loading, have been aborted, or have errors.

- **boolean isErrorAny()**

Returns true if any tracked image has an error.

- **Object[] getErrorsAny()**

Returns an array of images that have errors.

The following methods are used to wait for images to load:
- **void waitForAll() throws InterruptedException**
- **boolean waitForAll(long ms) throws InterruptedException**
- **void waitForID(int id) throws InterruptedException**
- **boolean waitForID(int id, long ms) throws InterruptedException**

These methods do not return until the tracked images have been loaded (or have encountered an error). The methods with an ms parameter wait until the images are finished or wait the number of microseconds specified by ms, whichever is shorter.

Menu Class

Several classes are used to make a menu for a program. An object of class **Menu** has **MenuItem** objects added to it, using methods in the **Menu** class. The menu can then be added to a frame by adding the **Menu** object to a **MenuBar** object and adding the menu bar to the frame. The Swing package (**javax.swing**) provides a lightweight version of this class called **JMenu**.

Constructors

- **Menu()**
- **Menu(String label)**
- **Menu(String label, boolean tearOff)**

The label of a menu is the text that will appear in the menu bar.

Methods

- **boolean isTearOff()**
- **int getItemCount()**
- **MenuItem getItem(int index)**
- **MenuItem add(MenuItem mi)**
- **void add(String label)**
- **void insert(MenuItem menuitem, int index)**
- **void insert(String label, int index)**

The methods used to add items to a menu either add the new item to the end of the menu or insert it at a specified index. Items can be added as a string or as a **MenuItem** object.

- **void addSeparator()**
- **void insertSeparator(int index)**

A separator is a line in the menu that is used to divide the menu items into different categories.

- **void remove(int index)**
- **void remove(MenuComponent item)**
- **void removeAll()**

MenuBar Class

The methods in the **MenuBar** class provide ways to add, remove, and access menus in a menu bar. To use a menu bar in a program, add it to a frame.

Constructors

- **MenuBar()**

Methods

- **Menu add(Menu m)**
- **void remove(int index)**
- **Menu getMenu(int i)**
- **int getMenuCount()**

MenuItem Class

When a user selects a menu item from a menu, the action listener associated with the menu item receives an action event. The program can determine which item was selected by matching the action command in the event object with the action command of a menu item.

The **PictureFrame** example in the **Complete Examples** section demonstrates the use of menu items with a pop-up menu.

Constructors

- **MenuItem()**
- **MenuItem(String label)**

Methods

- **void addActionListener(ActionListener l)**
- **void removeActionListener(ActionListener l)**
- **void setActionCommand(String command)**
- **String getActionCommand()**
- **void setShortcut(MenuShortcut s)**
- **void deleteShortcut()**

These two methods allow shortcuts to be associated with a menu item, or to delete a shortcut that is associated with a menu item.

MenuShortcut Class

A menu shortcut is a way for a menu item to be selected using the keyboard rather than the mouse. To provide a keyboard equivalent for a menu item, create a shortcut by using one of the constructors given below, and then use the **setShortcut** method of the **MenuItem** class to associate the shortcut with the menu item.

Constructors

- **MenuShortcut(int key)**
- **MenuShortcut(int key, boolean useShiftModifier)**

Methods

- **int getKey()**
- **boolean usesShiftModifier()**
- **boolean equals(MenuShortcut s)**

Panel Class

A panel is a container to which other components, including other panels, can be added. The methods most commonly used with panels are methods that are inherited from the **Container** or **Component** ancestor class.

Constructors

- **Panel()**
- **Panel(LayoutManager layout)**

Point Class

An object of the **Point** class contains two pieces of information: an **x** coordinate and a **y** coordinate.

Variables

- **int x**
- **int y**

Constructors

- **Point()**
This constructor makes a **Point** with coordinates $(0, 0)$.

- **Point(Point p)**
- **Point(int x, int y)**

Methods

- **double getX()**
- **double getY()**

- **void move(int nx, int ny)**

This method makes **nx** the new value of the **x** coordinate and **ny** the new value of the **y** coordinate.

- **void translate(int dx, int dy)**

This method adds **dx** to the **x** value of the **Point**, and adds **dy** to the **y** value of the **Point**.

- **boolean equals(Object obj)**

This method returns **true** if **obj** is a reference to a **Point** with equal values for **x** and **y**.

Polygon Class

A polygon is defined in terms of some number of points (vertices) connected by line segments. The points are in an ordered list, with a line segment connecting each point in the list to the next. The last point in the list is connected to the first point as well.

Variables

- **int npoints**
- **int[] xpoints**
- **int[] ypoints**
- **protected Rectangle bounds**

Constructors

- **Polygon()**

This constructor makes an empty polygon with no points in the list.

- **Polygon(int[] xpoints, int[] ypoints, int npoints)**

This constructor makes a new polygon where the **x** coordinate of each point comes from **xpoints** and the **y** coordinate comes from the corresponding element in **ypoints**. **npoints** tells how many points are in the polygon.

Methods

- **void translate(int dx, int dy)**

This method adds **dx** to the **x** coordinate of each point in the polygon and **dy** to the **y** coordinate of each point.

- **void addPoint(int x, int y)**

This method adds the point specified by the parameter to the end of the list as a new vertex of the polygon.

- **Rectangle getBounds()**

This method returns the smallest rectangle that contains the polygon and has sides parallel to the x and y axes.

- **boolean contains(Point p)**
- **boolean contains(int x, int y)**

This method returns **true** if the parameter(s) specify a point that is inside the polygon.

- **boolean contains(double x, double y, double w, double h)**
This method returns **true** if the parameters specify a rectangle that is inside the polygon.

- **boolean intersects(double x, double y, double w, double h)**
This method returns **true** if the rectangle specified by the parameters intersects the polygon.

PopupMenu Class

This class defines a menu that can be displayed anywhere in a component and, in contrast to **Menu** objects, does not have to be in a menu bar. The **PopupMenu** class inherits from the **Menu** class, so the methods that are used to add menu items to a **Menu** object can also be used with objects of this class.

The **PictureFrame** example in the **Complete Examples** section demonstrates the use of a pop-up menu.

Constructors

- **PopupMenu()**
- **PopupMenu(String label)**

Methods

- **void show(Component origin, int x, int y)**
This method shows the pop-up menu at a point specified by the **x** and **y** parameters to the method. The **x** and **y** coordinates are relative to the **origin** component. This method cannot be called if the pop-up menu is part of a menu bar.

Example The following code shows a simple example of a pop-up menu. The pop-up menu appears whenever the user clicks the mouse (left or right button). It has two menu items, one that says "Hello" and one that says "Good-bye." Note that the frame used in this example does not have a working close button for space reasons. See the description of the **Frame** class for an example of how to set up the close button.

```java
import java.awt.*;
import java.awt.event.*;

class FrameApp extends Frame implements MouseListener,
                                        ActionListener {
    private PopupMenu pop;
    private MenuItem item;
    public FrameApp () {
        addMouseListener(this);
        pop = new PopupMenu();
        item = new MenuItem("Hello");
        item.addActionListener(this);
```

```
            pop.add(item);
            item = new MenuItem("Good-bye");
            item.addActionListener(this);
            pop.add(item);
            add(pop);
        }
        public void actionPerformed(ActionEvent e) {
            System.out.println(e.getActionCommand());
        }
        public void mouseClicked(MouseEvent e) {}
        public void mouseEntered(MouseEvent e) {}
        public void mouseExited(MouseEvent e) {}
        public void mousePressed(MouseEvent e) {
            pop.show(e.getComponent(), e.getX(), e.getY());
        }
        public void mouseReleased(MouseEvent e) {}
        public static void main(String[] args) {
            FrameApp win = new FrameApp();
            win.setSize(300, 200);
            win.show();
        }
    }
```

Rectangle Class

A rectangle is specified by its upper-left corner, its height, and its width.

Variables

- `public int x`
- `public int y`
- `public int width`
- `public int height`

The **x** and **y** coordinates are for the upper-left corner of the rectangle.

Constructors

- `Rectangle()`
- `Rectangle(Rectangle r)`
- `Rectangle(int x, int y, int width, int height)`
- `Rectangle(int width, int height)`
- `Rectangle(Point p, Dimension d)`
- `Rectangle(Point p)`
- `Rectangle(Dimension d)`

Constructors that do not specify **x** and **y** coordinates (or a **Point**) make a rectangle with an upper-left corner of (0,0). Constructors that do not specify a width or height make a rectangle with width and height of zero.

Methods

- **double getX()**
- **double getY()**
- **double getWidth()**
- **double getHeight()**
- **void setLocation(Point p)**
- **void setLocation(int x, int y)**
- **void setSize(Dimension d)**
- **void setSize(int width, int height)**
- **void translate(int dx, int dy)**

This method adds **dx** to the **x** coordinate and **dy** to the **y** coordinate. If **dx** and **dy** are both positive, the rectangle will move to the right and down.

- **boolean contains(Point p)**
- **boolean contains(int x, int y)**

This method returns **true** if the rectangle contains the point specified by the parameter(s).

- **boolean contains(Rectangle r)**
- **boolean contains(int x, int y, int w, int h)**

This method returns **true** if the rectangle contains the rectangle specified by the parameter(s).

- **boolean isEmpty()**

This method returns **true** if the rectangle has a height or width that is zero or less.

- **boolean equals(Object obj)**

This method returns **true** if the rectangle has the same **x** and **y** coordinates as the parameter, and the rectangle has the same width and height as the parameter.

Scrollbar Class

The following table shows the properties of scrollbar components and their default values:

Property	Description	Default value
Orientation	Vertical or horizontal	**Scrollbar.VERTICAL**
Value	Location of scroll bar bubble	0
Minimum	Minimum value	0
Maximum	Maximum value	100
Unit increment	Change in value when the up or down arrow is clicked or when the up or down arrow key is pressed	1
Block increment	change in value when the scroll bar track is clicked or when the Page Up or Page Down key is pressed	10

Each of these properties has methods to get and set its value.

Constants

- `static final int HORIZONTAL`
- `static final int VERTICAL`

Constructors

- `Scrollbar()`
- `Scrollbar(int orientation)`
- `Scrollbar(int orientation, int value, int visible,`
  `                 int minimum, int maximum)`

Methods

- `int getOrientation()`
- `void setOrientation(int orientation)`
- `void setUnitIncrement(int v)`
- `int getUnitIncrement()`
- `void setBlockIncrement(int v)`
- `int getBlockIncrement()`
- `int getValue()`
- `int getVisibleAmount()`
- `int getMinimum()`
- `int getMaximum()`
- `void setValues(int value, int visible,`
  `                 int minimum, int maximum)`

These properties should be set at the same time to ensure that they are consistent. Setting the amount of visible material tells the object what range of values between minimum and maximum is currently displayed.

- `void addAdjustmentListener(AdjustmentListener l)`
- `void removeAdjustmentListener(AdjustmentListener l)`

ScrollPane Class

A `ScrollPane` object is a container that can contain a single child component. The scroll pane automatically provides scrollbars for the user to move the display. The scrollbars are displayed according to the display policy, which can be as needed, always, or never. Access to the scrollbars is provided through two methods which return **Adjustable** objects. The **Adjustable** interface provides the same kind of constants and methods as are used by the **Scrollbar** class.

Constants

- `static final int SCROLLBARS_AS_NEEDED`
- `static final int SCROLLBARS_ALWAYS`
- `static final int SCROLLBARS_NEVER`

These constants are used to set the policy for scrollbars on the pane. If the constant **SCROLLBARS_AS_NEEDED** constant is used, the scrollbars are displayed only if the child is too big to be displayed all at once.

Constructors

- **ScrollPane()**
- **ScrollPane(int policy)**

The value of the policy parameter should be one of the three constants listed above, which indicate whether the scrollbars should sometimes (as needed), always, or never be displayed.

Methods

- **protected final void addImpl(Component comp, Object constraints, int index)**

This method is the way to add the child display to the scroll pane. The first parameter is the component that will be scrolled. The second parameter is not used. The third parameter should be less than or equal to zero.

- **int getScrollbarDisplayPolicy()**
- **Dimension getViewportSize()**

This method returns the size of the viewport in pixels.

- **int getHScrollbarHeight()**
- **int getVScrollbarWidth()**

These two methods return the height and width, respectively, of the scrollbars, regardless of whether the scrollbars are actually displayed.

- **Adjustable getVAdjustable()**
- **Adjustable getHAdjustable()**

These two methods provide access to the scrollbars, since the **Adjustable** interface provides the same types of constants and methods as the **Scrollbar** class.

- **void setScrollPosition(int x, int y)**
- **void setScrollPosition(Point p)**

These methods scroll to the position in the child component that is specified by the parameter(s). This is an alternative to using the **getVAdjustable** and **getHAdjustable** methods.

- **Point getScrollPosition()**

This method returns the scroll position of the child component. The same information may be obtained by using the **getVAdjustable** and **getHAdjustable** methods.

TextArea Class

A text area is a component that can display more than one line of text. It can be set to allow or not allow user editing of the text. The component automatically provides scrollbars, and provides constants and methods to make the scrollbars visible or not.

The Swing package contains a lightweight version of this component that is called **JTextArea**.

Constants

- **static final int SCROLLBARS_BOTH**
- **static final int SCROLLBARS_VERTICAL_ONLY**
- **static final int SCROLLBARS_HORIZONTAL_ONLY**
- **static final int SCROLLBARS_NONE**

Constructors

- **TextArea()**
- **TextArea(String text)**
- **TextArea(int rows, int columns)**
- **TextArea(String text, int rows, int columns)**
- **TextArea(String text, int rows, int columns, int scrollbars)**

The last constructor is the only method that provides a way to set the visibility of the scrollbars. All the other constructors default to both visible scrollbars.

Methods

- **void insert(String str, int pos)**

The **pos** parameter tells the position (character offset) in the text area where the **str** parameter text should be inserted.

- **void append(String str)**

This method adds the **str** parameter to the end of the text in the text area.

- **void replaceRange(String str, int start, int end)**

This method replaces the text in the text area from position (character offset) **start** to **end** with the text in the parameter **str**.

- **int getRows()**
- **void setRows(int rows)**
- **int getColumns()**
- **void setColumns(int columns)**
- **int getScrollbarVisibility()**
- **Dimension getPreferredSize()**
- **Dimension getMinimumSize()**
- **Dimension getPreferredSize(int rows, int columns)**
- **Dimension getMinimumSize(int rows, int columns)**

The last two methods provide a way to convert dimensions in characters to dimensions in pixels.

Note that the **TextArea** class inherits methods from the **TextComponent** class, including methods for working with text listeners and text selections.

TextField Class

A text field is used to allow a user to view and edit a single line of text. If a text field has an action listener added to it, the listener will receive an **ActionEvent** when the user presses the Enter key. By setting an echo character, a program can hide the user's input.

Constructors

- `TextField()`
- `TextField(String text)`
- `TextField(int columns)`
- `TextField(String text, int columns)`

Methods

- `char getEchoChar()`
- `void setEchoChar(char c)`
- `boolean echoCharIsSet()`

If the echo character is not set, or is set to zero, user input will be echoed normally in the text field. If the echo character is set to some value other than zero, the echo character will be displayed instead of each character the user enters.

- `void setText(String t)`
- `String getText()`

The `getText` method is inherited from the `TextComponent` class.

- `int getColumns()`
- `void setColumns(int columns)`

A column is an approximate average character width.

- `Dimension getPreferredSize(int columns)`
- `Dimension getPreferredSize()`
- `Dimension getMinimumSize(int columns)`
- `Dimension getMinimumSize()`

- `void addActionListener(ActionListener l)`
- `void removeActionListener(ActionListener l)`

Note that in addition to inheriting the `getText` method from the `TextComponent` class, `TextField` also inherits methods for dealing with text selections and text listeners.

Toolkit Class

The `Toolkit` class is abstract, so it cannot be instantiated directly. The most common use of the class is to use the static method `getDefaultToolkit`. Using the default toolkit, an application can get images using the `getImage` method.

Methods

- **static Toolkit getDefaultToolkit()**

This static method is used to a get a toolkit which is not abstract.

- **abstract Image getImage(String filename)**
- **abstract Image getImage(URL url)**

These methods are listed as abstract in the **Toolkit** class, but are implemented in descendant classes and can be called from the object returned by **getDefault-Toolkit**. These methods cache images, and this may result in an image being kept longer than necessary. The **createImage** method does a similar job but without caching.

- **abstract Image createImage(String filename)**
- **abstract Image createImage(URL url)**

These methods are similar to **getImage**, but do not cache images.

An application can use this class to get an image by using code like the following:

```
Image pic;
pic = Toolkit.getDefaultToolkit().getImage("sheep.jpg");
```

Window Class

The **Window** class can be used to draw a window on the screen that has no frame and no menu. Generally it will be used by inheritance rather than directly in a program. A window has a frame or another window as an owner. A window is made visible by using the **show** method. The Swing package contains a lightweight window class called **JWindow**.

Constructors

- **Window(Frame owner)**
- **Window(Window owner)**
- **Window(Window owner, GraphicsConfiguration gc)**

Methods

- **void show()**

This method validates and displays the window. If the window is already visible, this method will bring it to the front.

- **void hide()**

This method hides the window so that it is not visible on the screen.

- **void pack()**

This method sizes the window, lays out its components, and makes it ready to be displayed.

- **void dispose()**

This method releases some of the memory and resources used by the window and marks the window as undisplayable. A subsequent call to pack or show will make the window displayable again.

- **void toFront()**

This method brings the window to the front.

- **void toBack()**

This method sends the window to the back.

- **Window getOwner()**

This method returns the owner of the window, which could be a window or a subclass of **Window**, such as a frame.

- **Window[] getOwnedWindows()**

This method returns an array of windows that this window owns.

- **void addWindowListener(WindowListener listener)**
- **void removeWindowListener(WindowListener listener)**
- **Component getFocusOwner()**

This method returns the child component that has focus.

Here is a small example of a class that extends the **Window** class:

```
class Win extends Window {
    private Image pic;

    public Win(Frame f) {
      super(f);
    }

    public void setPic(Image i) {
      pic = i;
    }

    public void paint(Graphics g) {
      g.drawImage(pic, 0, 0, this);
    }
}
```

Note that this class cannot compile unless it has a constructor defined, because **Window** does not have a no-argument constructor that will be called by default.

java.awt.event Package

This package includes interfaces for different kinds of listeners as well as classes for different kinds of events. It also includes adapters, which are classes that implement all of the methods for an interface but do nothing to process events.

All the methods listed for an interface must be defined in order for a class to implement the interface. So, for example, a class must define the **ActionPerformed** method to be used as an **ActionListener**, and a class must define all six methods listed in the **WindowListener** interface in order to be used as a **WindowListener**.

Adapters are convenient because they allow a class to define only the methods of interest and use the inherited methods for the rest. For instance, in order to implement the **WindowListener** interface, six methods must be defined even if only one is actually being used. If the class inherits from the **WindowAdapter** class, only the method of interest must be defined, and the rest of the methods will be available from the parent class.

For the descriptions of adapter classes, the methods are listed without description. For a description of how the methods are used, refer to the corresponding listener interface.

Every class in this section that has **Event** in its name extends the **AWTEvent** class, and every interface with **Listener** in its name extends the **EventListener** interface.

Constructors of events are not usually used directly and so are not listed here.

ActionEvent Class

Constants

- static final int SHIFT_MASK
- static final int CTRL_MASK
- static final int META_MASK
- static final int ALT_MASK

Methods

- **String getActionCommand()**

This method returns the command associated with the event that has occurred. The action command for a component (like a button) can be set explicitly, but the default will be the label of the button.

- **int getModifiers()**

This method is used to tell which modifiers (such as holding down the Shift key) were used with this event. The value it returns can be used with the bitwise AND operator (&) and the mask constants to tell which modifiers apply to this event.

ActionListener Interface

Methods

- **void actionPerformed(ActionEvent e)**

This method tells the listener that an action has occurred. Information about the action can be obtained from the **ActionEvent** object passed as the parameter.

ItemEvent Class

This type of event occurs when an item is selected or deselected in a component such as a list.

Constants

- static final int SELECTED
- static final int DESELECTED

Methods

- **ItemSelectable getItemSelectable()**

This method returns the object that generated the event.

* `Object getItem()`

This method returns the item that was selected or deselected by the event.

* `int getStateChange()`

This method tells whether the item was selected or deselected by returning **SELECTED** or **DESELECTED**.

ItemListener Interface

* `void itemStateChanged(ItemEvent e)`

This method informs the listener that an item has been selected or deselected.

KeyAdapter Class

A class that extends the **KeyAdapter** class defines methods to override one or more of these inherited methods. If all three of these methods are being used, the class would normally be declared as implementing the **KeyListener** interface rather than extending the **KeyAdapter** class.

Methods

* `void keyTyped(KeyEvent e)`
* `void keyPressed(KeyEvent e)`
* `void keyReleased(KeyEvent e)`

See the **KeyListener** interface for descriptions of these methods.

KeyEvent Class

This class defines numerous constants used to indicate which key was pressed. Most of the key names are self-explanatory and therefore are not described. Not all of the constants defined in the class are listed here. Some constants (for the digits and the letters of the alphabet) are listed as ranges.

The **SpotlightApplet** example in the **Complete Examples** section shows one way to use the **KeyEvent** class and the constants defined in it.

Constants

* `VK_0` through `VK_9`

These constants represent the keys for the digits zero through nine. These constants are the same as ASCII '0' through ASCII '9'.

* `VK_A` through `VK_Z`

These constants represent the keys for the letters A through Z. They are the same as ASCII 'A' through ASCII 'Z'.

* `VK_DOWN, VK_UP, VK_LEFT, VK_RIGHT`

These are the constants used for the arrow keys.

* `VK_F1` through `VK_F24`

These are the constants for the function keys.

* `VK_NUMPAD0` through `VK_NUMPAD9`

These constants represent the number pad keys for the digits zero through nine.

- `VK_KP_UP, VK_KP_DOWN, VK_KP_LEFT, VK_KP_RIGHT`

These are constants for the arrows on the key pad.

The following are constants for some of the punctuation symbols and non-alphanumeric keys.

- `VK_ADD`
- `VK_ALT`
- `VK_AMPERSAND`
- `VK_ASTERISK`
- `VK_AT`
- `VK_BACK_QUOTE`
- `VK_BACK_SLASH`
- `VK_BACK_SPACE`
- `VK_BRACELEFT`
- `VK_BRACERIGHT`
- `VK_CANCEL`
- `VK_CAPS_LOCK`
- `VK_CIRCUMFLEX`
- `VK_CLEAR`
- `VK_CLOSE_BRACKET`
- `VK_COLON`
- `VK_COMMA`
- `VK_CONTROL`
- `VK_DECIMAL`
- `VK_DELETE`
- `VK_DIVIDE`
- `VK_DOLLAR`
- `VK_END`
- `VK_ENTER`
- `VK_EQUALS`
- `VK_ESCAPE`
- `VK_EURO_SIGN`
- `VK_EXCLAMATION_MARK`
- `VK_GREATER`

- `VK_HELP`
- `VK_HOME`
- `VK_INSERT`
- `VK_INVERTED_EXCLAMATION_MARK`
- `VK_LEFT_PARENTHESIS`
- `VK_LESS`
- `VK_MINUS`
- `VK_MULTIPLY`
- `VK_NUM_LOCK`
- `VK_NUMBER_SIGN`
- `VK_OPEN_BRACKET`
- `VK_PAGE_DOWN`
- `VK_PAGE_UP`
- `VK_PAUSE`
- `VK_PERIOD`
- `VK_PLUS`
- `VK_PRINTSCREEN`
- `VK_QUOTE`
- `VK_QUOTEDBL`
- `VK_RIGHT_PARENTHESIS`
- `VK_SCROLL_LOCK`
- `VK_SEMICOLON`
- `VK_SEPARATER`
- `VK_SHIFT`
- `VK_SLASH`
- `VK_SPACE`
- `VK_SUBTRACT`
- `VK_TAB`
- `VK_UNDERSCORE`

Methods

- `int getKeyCode()`

This method tells the key associated with this event. The **VK** constants listed above can be used to determine the key for the event.

- **char getKeyChar()**

This method returns the Unicode character for the key associated with the event. Note that not every key has a character associated with it. For instance, the Enter key does not.

- **static String getKeyText(int keyCode)**

This method returns a string describing the key code. For example, the string **"ENTER"** describes the **VK_ENTER** key code.

KeyListener Interface

This listener interface is used for events that occur when a user presses keys on the keyboard.

Methods

- **void keyTyped(KeyEvent e)**

This method is called when the user has pressed and released a key.

- **void keyPressed(KeyEvent e)**
- **void keyReleased(KeyEvent e)**

MouseAdapter Class

A class that extends the **MouseAdapter** class defines methods to override one or more of these inherited methods. If all five of these methods are being used, the class would normally be declared as implementing the **MouseListener** interface rather than extending the **MouseAdapter** class.

Methods

- **void mouseClicked(MouseEvent e)**
- **void mouseEntered(MouseEvent e)**
- **void mouseExited(MouseEvent e)**
- **void mousePressed(MouseEvent e)**
- **void mouseReleased(MouseEvent e)**

See the **MouseListener** interface description for an explanation of these methods.

MouseEvent Class

This type of event includes information about events that occur when the user presses and/or releases a mouse button.

Methods

- **int getX()**
- **int getY()**
- **Point getPoint()**

These methods provide the location of a mouse button click, either as separate **x** (horizontal) and **y** (vertical) coordinates, or as a **Point**.

- **int getClickCount()**

This method tells how many times the mouse button was pressed.

The following constants and methods, inherited from **InputEvent**, are useful in determining which mouse button was pressed (or released):

Constants

- **static final int BUTTON1_MASK**
- **static final int BUTTON2_MASK**
- **static final int BUTTON3_MASK**

Methods

- **int getModifiers()**

MouseMotionAdapter Class

A class that extends the **MouseMotionAdapter** class defines methods to override one or more of these inherited methods. If both of these methods are being used, the class would normally be declared as implementing the **MouseMotionListener** interface rather than extending the **MouseMotionAdapter** class.

Methods

- **void mouseDragged(MouseEvent e)**
- **void mouseMoved(MouseEvent e)**

See the **MouseMotionListener** interface description for an explanation of these methods.

MouseMotionListener Interface

This listener interface is used with events that occur when the user moves or drags the mouse.

Methods

- **void mouseDragged(MouseEvent e)**

This method is called when the mouse is moved with with a button held down.

- **void mouseMoved(MouseEvent e)**

This method is called when the mouse is moved with within the boundaries of a component that has a **MouseMotionListener** associated with it.

MouseListener Interface

This listener interface is used with events that occur when the user presses and/or releases a mouse button.

Methods

- **void mouseClicked(MouseEvent e)**

This method is called when a mouse button is pressed and released.

- **void mouseEntered(MouseEvent e)**

This method is called when the mouse is moved into the area of a component that has a **MouseListener** associated with it.

- **void mouseExited(MouseEvent e)**

This method is called when the mouse is moved out of the area of a component that has a **MouseListener** associated with it.

- **void mousePressed(MouseEvent e)**

This method is called when a mouse button is pressed.

- **void mouseReleased(MouseEvent e)**

This method is called when a mouse button is released.

TextEvent Class

This type of event occurs when the user changes the text in a component such as a text area or text field.

Methods

- **Object getSource()**

This inherited method can be used to find out which component's text has been changed.

WindowAdapter Class

A class that extends the **WindowAdapter** class defines methods to override one or more of these inherited methods. If all six of these methods are being used, the class would normally be declared as implementing the **WindowListener** interface rather than extending the **WindowAdapter** class.

Methods

- **void windowOpened(WindowEvent e)**
- **void windowClosing(WindowEvent e)**
- **void windowClosed(WindowEvent e)**
- **void windowIconified(WindowEvent e)**
- **void windowDeiconified(WindowEvent e)**
- **void windowActivated(WindowEvent e)**

See the description of the **WindowListener** interface for descriptions of these methods.

WindowEvent Class

This type of event occurs when a window is opened, closed, iconified, deiconified, or activated. It also occurs when the user attempts to close the window.

Methods

- **Window getWindow()**

This method tells which window is associated with the event.

WindowListener Interface

This listener interface is used with window events. The most commonly used method is the `windowClosing` method, which can be used to end a program when the user clicks the close box of the window.

Methods

- **void windowOpened(WindowEvent e)**
This method is called when a window is first displayed on the screen.

- **void windowClosing(WindowEvent e)**
This method is called when the user does an action to close a window (for example, clicking on a close button or choosing close from a system menu). The window will not actually close unless the program hides or disposes the window when this method is called.

- **void windowClosed(WindowEvent e)**
This method is called when the window has been closed.

- **void windowIconified(WindowEvent e)**
This method is called when the window has been iconified. An iconified window is no longer displayed on the screen. Instead there is a small representation of it (an icon) that can be used to display the window again.

- **void windowDeiconified(WindowEvent e)**
This method is called when a window that has been iconified is no longer iconified.

- **void windowActivated(WindowEvent e)**

java.io Package

I/O classes in Java fall into the categories of input or output, of course (hence the name I/O for Input/Output), but they also differ in that they can be used either with characters or with bytes. Classes that have **Reader** or **Writer** in their name are used with characters. Classes that have **InputStream** or **OutputStream** in their name are used with bytes. If your program is working with text, you will probably want to use the **Reader**/**Writer** classes. On the other hand, if your program is working with binary data, such as an image file, you will probably want to use the **InputStream**/**OutputStream** classes.

Since reading a small amount of data takes nearly as much time as reading a larger amount of data, it is more efficient to read large amounts of data. Some I/O classes make I/O more efficient by providing buffering, which is a way to read (or write) large amounts of data at once. When your program calls the **read** method from the **BufferedReader** class, for instance, the buffered reader reads a large amount of data into its buffer. Then, on the next call to **read**, it may be able return information from the buffer instead of having to do another read for a small amount of data. When the buffer is empty, the buffered reader reads from the input stream again. Buffers are also used in output classes.

In some cases, a constructor for one class will take an object of another class as a parameter. For example, a **BufferedReader** constructor can take a **FileReader** object as its parameter.

BufferedInputStream Class

This class adds buffering to its ancestor class, **InputStream**.

Constructors

- **BufferedInputStream(InputStream in)**
- **BufferedInputStream(InputStream in, int size)**

Methods

- **int read() throws IOException**
- **int read(byte[] b, int off, int len) throws IOException**
- **long skip(long n) throws IOException**
- **int available() throws IOException**

BufferedReader Class

This class provides buffered input from a character stream. The **PageWriter** example in the **Complete Examples** section uses a **BufferedReader** to read from a file.

Constructors

- **BufferedReader(Reader in)**
This constructor creates a buffered reader for the reader passed in as a parameter. Often the **Reader** parameter is an **InputStreamReader** object or a **FileReader** object.

- **BufferedReader(Reader in, int sz)**
This constructor makes a buffered reader that has a buffer of size **sz**.

Methods

- **int read() throws IOException**
This method reads one character.

- **abstract int read(char[] inBuff, int offset, int len)**
                                      throws IOException
This method reads up to **len** characters and stores them in **inBuff**, beginning at index **offset**.

- **String readLine() throws IOException**
This method reads a line of text. A line of text is terminated by a newline character ('\n'), a carriage return ('\r'), or both together. The terminating characters are not included in the string returned by the method.

- **long skip(long n) throws IOException**
This method skips **n** characters in the input stream.

- **`void close() throws IOException`**

This method closes the stream.

A common way to read from the keyboard is to make an **`InputStreamReader`** using **`System`**.in, and then pass that reader to the **`BufferedReader`** constructor, as follows:

```
BufferedReader in
    = new BufferedReader(new InputStreamReader(System.in));
```

The program can then use the **`readLine`** method of **`BufferedReader`** to read **`String`** objects from the keyboard.

BufferedWriter Class

This class provides buffered output to a character stream.

Constructors

- **`BufferedWriter(Writer out)`**

- **`BufferedWriter(Writer out, int sz)`**

This method creates a buffered writer with a buffer of size **`sz`**.

Methods

- **`void write(int c) throws IOException`**

This method writes one character.

- **`void write(char[] outBuff, int offset, int len)`**
                                     `throws IOException`

This method writes **`len`** characters, beginning at index **`offset`** in the array **`out-Buff`**, and stores them in **`outBuff`**.

- **`void newLine() throws IOException`**

This method writes a newline character, or the equivalent, to the character output stream.

- **`void newLine() throws IOException`**

This method flushes the output stream.

FileInputStream Class

This class provides a way to read data from a file. Its parent class is **`InputStream`**.

Constructors

- **`protected FileInputStream(File file)`**

- **`protected FileInputStream(String fileName)`**

Methods

- **`int read() throws IOException`**
- **`int read(byte[] b) throws IOException`**
- **`int read(byte[] b, int off, int len) throws IOException`**

- `long skip(long n) throws IOException`
- `int available() throws IOException`
- `void close() throws IOException`
- `void mark(int readlimit)`
- `void reset() throws IOException`

FileOutputStream Class

This class provides a way to write data to a file. Its parent class is `OutputStream`.

Constructors

- `FileOutputStream(OutputStream out)`
- `FileOutputStream(String fileName)`

Methods

- `void write(int b) throws IOException`
- `void write(byte[] b) throws IOException`
- `void write(byte[] b, int off, int len) throws IOException`
- `void flush() throws IOException`
- `void close() throws IOException`

FileReader Class

This class provides character input from a file. A file reader is often passed as a parameter to the constructor of the `BufferedReader` class. The `PageWriter` example in the **Complete Examples** section shows an example of using a `FileReader` object.

Constructors

- `FileReader(String fileName) throws FileNotFoundException`
- `FileReader(File file) throws FileNotFoundException`
- `FileReader(FileDescriptor fd)`
  The only methods in this class are inherited from its ancestor classes: `InputStreamReader`, `Reader`, and `Object`.

FileWriter Class

This class provides character output to a file. A file reader is often passed as a parameter to the constructor of the `PrintWriter` class. The `PageWriter` example in the **Complete Examples** section shows an example of using a `FileWriter` object.

Constructors

- `FileWriter(String fileName)`
- `FileWriter(File file)`
- `FileWriter(FileDescriptor fd)`
  The only methods in this class are inherited from its ancestor classes: `OutputStreamWriter`, `Writer`, and `Object`.

InputStream Class

This is an abstract class, so it cannot be directly instantiated. Instead, it provides a base for inheritance. All classes that input bytes (rather than text or characters) inherit from this class.

Constructors

- `InputStream()`

Methods

- `abstract int read() throws IOException`
A descendant class must implement this method or be abstract. This method returns the next byte from the input stream. The return value is an integer in the range of 0–255, unless no more input is available, in which case the return value will be –1.

InputStreamReader Class

This class reads bytes from an input stream and translates them into characters. The parent class of `InputStreamReader` is the `Reader` class. The corresponding output class is `OutputStreamWriter`, which takes characters and writes them to a byte output stream.

Constructors

- `InputStreamReader(InputStream in)`
This constructor creates a reader that uses the default character encoding scheme to translate bytes to characters.

Methods

- `int read() throws IOException`
This method returns one character from the input stream or –1 if there is nothing more to read from the stream.

- `int read(char[] buffer, int off, int len) throws IOException`
This method reads at most `len` characters and puts them in the array `buffer`, beginning at offset `off`.

ObjectInputStream Class

This class, together with `ObjectOutputStream`, is used for object serialization. Object serialization means to put an object into a form that can be written to a file or sent to another computer via a network connection.

Constructors

- `ObjectInputStream(InputStream in) throws IOException,`
                                    `StreamCorruptedException`
A `FileInputStream` is one example of an input stream that can be passed as a parameter to this constructor.

Methods

> • `Object readObject() throws OptionalDataException,`
> `                        ClassNotFoundException, IOException`
> This method reads an object from the input stream. The return value should be cast to the class of object that is read in.

ObjectOutputStream Class

This class is used for object serialization (see the description for `ObjectInput-Stream`). It includes various methods for writing information to the stream, but `writeObject` is the method that differs the most from the output methods available in other classes.

Constructors

> • `ObjectOutputStream(OutputStream out) throws IOException`
> Note that this constructor takes an output stream as its parameter. A `FileOutputStream` object is one type of object that could be passed as the parameter.

Methods

> • `void writeObject(Object obj) throws IOException`
> The `obj` parameter must be an object of a class that implements the `Serializable` interface. The `Serializable` interface does not include any methods, so a class can implement simply by including "`implements Serializable`" in the class definition.

OutputStream Class

This is an abstract class, so it cannot be directly instantiated. Instead, it provides a base for inheritance. All classes that output bytes (rather than text or characters) inherit from this class.

Constructors

> • `OutputStream()`

Methods

> • `abstract void write(int b) throws IOException`
> The 24 high-order bits of the parameter `b` are ignored. A descendant class must implement this method if it is not abstract.

OutputStreamWriter Class

This class takes characters and writes them to a byte output stream. The parent class of `OutputStreamWriter` is the `Writer` class. The corresponding output class is `InputStreamReader`, which takes characters and writes them to a byte output stream.

Constructors

- **OutputStreamWriter(OutputStream out)**

This constructor creates a writer that uses the default character-encoding scheme to translate characters to bytes.

Methods

- **void write(int c) throws IOException**

This method writes one character to the input stream.

- **void write(char[] buffer, int off, int len) throws IOException**

This method writes **len** characters from the array **buffer**, beginning at offset **off**.

- **void write(String str, int off, int len) throws IOException**

This method writes **len** characters from the string **str**, beginning at offset **off**.

PrintStream Class

This class provides formatted output of data. Since it is a descendant of **OutputStream**, it writes bytes rather than 16-bit characters. Characters are converted to bytes using the default encoding, or in other words, the default way to convert 16-bit Unicode characters to 8-bit characters.

Note that the methods in this class do not cause I/O exceptions. Instead, the program must use the **checkError** method to see if an error has occurred.

Constructors

- **PrintStream(OutputStream out)**
- **PrintStream(OutputStream out, boolean autoFlush)**

If the **autoflush** parameter is **true**, the stream's buffer will be flushed when the **println** method is called.

Methods

- **void flush()**
- **void close()**
- **boolean checkError()**

This method returns true if an error has occurred. This method is necessary because the methods in this class do not throw I/O exceptions.

- **void print(boolean b)**
- **void print(char c)**
- **void print(char[] s)**
- **void print(int i)**
- **void print(long l)**
- **void print(float f)**
- **void print(double d)**

- **void print(String s)**
- **void print(Object obj)**

The **toString** method of **obj** will be called to get a string which can be printed. Since the default **toString** method inherited from **Object** won't always be useful, you will usually want to include a **toString** method in your classes that returns a useful **String** representation of the class's objects.

The various **println** methods will terminate the line after printing their parameter.

- **void println()**
- **void println(boolean b)**
- **void println(char c)**
- **void println(char[] s)**
- **void println(int i)**
- **void println(long l)**
- **void println(float f)**
- **void println(double d)**
- **void println(String s)**
- **PrintStream printf(String s)**

This method takes a format string as its first parameter and a variable number of other objects as additional parameters. The format string has a placeholder that tells how each additional value should be printed.

Examples of placeholders are **%s** for a string, **%d** for an integer, and **%f** for a double. In addition to placeholders, the format string can contain literal characters that will be printed as they appear in the string.

Format strings can be quite complicated. For a complete description, see the Java API description for the class **Formatter** in the package **java.util** (Java 1.5 and later). If you want to use a format string without printing anything, you can use the static method **format** in the **String** class.

The following code shows an example of a method call for **printf**:

```
int count = 5;
String item = "strawberries";
System.out.printf("I picked %d %s today.\n", count, item);
```

The preceding code gives the following output:

```
I picked 5 strawberries today.
```

PrintWriter Class

This class provides formatted character output. Note that the methods in this class do not cause I/O exceptions. Instead, the program must use the **checkError** method to see if an error has occurred. The **PageWriter** example in the **Complete Examples** section shows an example of using a **FileWriter** object.

Constructors

- **PrintWriter(Writer out)**
- **PrintWriter(Writer out, boolean autoFlush)**

- `PrintWriter(OutputStream out)`
- `PrintWriter(OutputStream out, boolean autoFlush)`

If the `autoflush` parameter is `true`, the stream's buffer will be flushed when the `println` method is called.

Methods

- `void flush()`
- `void close()`
- `boolean checkError()`

This method returns `true` if an error has occurred. This method is necessary because the methods in this class do not throw I/O exceptions.

- `void print(boolean b)`
- `void print(char c)`
- `void print(int i)`
- `void print(long l)`
- `void print(float f)`
- `void print(double d)`
- `void print(char[] s)`
- `void print(String s)`
- `void print(Object obj)`

The `toString` method of `obj` will be called to get a string which can be printed. Since the default `toString` method inherited from `Object` won't always be useful, you will usually want to include a `toString` method in your classes that returns a useful `String` representation of the class's objects.

The various `println` methods will terminate the line after printing their parameters.

- `void println()`
- `void println(boolean b)`
- `void println(char c)`
- `void println(int i)`
- `void println(long l)`
- `void println(float f)`
- `void println(double d)`
- `void println(char[] s)`
- `void println(String s)`

Reader Class

Since `Reader` is an abstract class, it cannot be instantiated. Its purpose is to provide a base which other classes can extend. Descendants of the `Reader` class are used for input from character streams.

Any descendant of **Reader** that is not abstract will include the following two methods:

Methods

- **abstract int read(char[] inBuff, int offset, int len)**
  throws IOException
  This method reads up to **len** characters and stores them in **inBuff**, beginning at index **offset**.

- **abstract void close() throws IOException**
  This method closes the stream. Further attempts to use a closed stream will cause an **IOException**.

Writer Class

Like **Reader**, **Writer** is an abstract class; it cannot be instantiated. Its purpose is to provide a base which other classes can extend. Descendants of the **Writer** class are used for output to character streams.

Any descendant of **Writer** that is not abstract will include the following three methods:

Methods

- **abstract void write(char[] outBuff, int offset, int len)**
  throws IOException
  This method writes **len** characters, beginning at index **offset** in the array **outBuff**, and stores them in **outBuff**.

- **abstract void close() throws IOException**
  This method closes the stream. Further attempts to use a closed stream will cause an **IOException**.

- **abstract void flush() throws IOException**
  This method writes the contents of any buffers that have not yet been written, and clears the buffers.

java.lang Package

This package includes commonly used classes like **String** and **Math**. You do not need to import the classes in this package to use them.

java.lang includes wrapper classes, which are classes that can be used to represent primitive-type values such as **int** or **char**. Wrapper classes provide usual conversion methods, such as **valueOf** and **toString**, and **parseInt** (and other parsing methods).

As of version 1.5 of Java, wrapper classes have been easier to work with because of the autoboxing and auto-unboxing feature. With autoboxing you don't need to use the constructor to copy a primitive value into a wrapper class object. Instead of using a line like this:

```
Integer countObj = new Integer(count);
```

you can simply use a line like this:

```
Integer countObj = count;
```

With auto-unboxing, you don't have to explicitly call a method to convert from a wrapper-class object to a primitive type. In the following example, **countObj** is an object of the **Integer** wrapper class. Without auto-unboxing, you must use the **intValue** method like this:

```
int count = countObj.intValue();
```

Using auto-unboxing, you don't have to explicitly call the conversion method:

```
int count = countObj;
```

Boolean Class

This is the wrapper class for the primitive type **boolean**.

Constants

- **static final Boolean TRUE**
- **static final Boolean FALSE**

The **Boolean** objects representing the primitive values **true** and **false**, respectively.

Constructors

- **Boolean(boolean value)**

This constructor makes an object that corresponds to the primitive value passed in as the parameter.

- **Boolean(String s)**

This constructor makes an object representing the value **true** if **s** is equal to **"true"** (ignoring case).

Methods

- **boolean booleanValue()**

This method returns the value of the object as a value of the primitive type **boolean**.

- **static Boolean valueOf(String s)**

This method returns a **Boolean** object that represents **true** if the string **s** is equal to **"true"** (ignoring case) and otherwise returns an object with the value **false**.

- **String toString()**

This method returns a **String** object representing the object's value, either **"true"** or **"false"**.

- **boolean equals(Object obj)**

This method returns **true** if **obj** is a **Boolean** object that represents the same value as the calling object.

Byte Class

This is the wrapper class for the primitive type **byte**.

Constants

- **static final Byte MAX_VALUE**
- **static final Byte MIN_VALUE**

The **Byte** objects representing the maximum and minimum values that a **byte** can have.

Constructors

- **Byte(byte value)**

This constructor makes an object that corresponds to the primitive value passed in as the parameter.

- **Byte(String s)**

This constructor makes an object representing the value passed in by the **String** parameter.

Methods

- **byte byteValue()**

This method returns the value of the object as a value of the primitive type **byte**.

- **static Byte valueOf(String s)**

This method returns a **Byte** object that has the value represented by the String parameter.

- **String toString()**

This method returns a **String** object representing the object's value.

- **boolean equals(Object obj)**

This method returns **true** if **obj** is a **Byte** object that represents the same value as the calling object.

- **static Byte decode(String num) throws NumberFormatException**

If the string **num** begins with **0x**, **0X**, or **#**, the number will be considered a hexadecimal (base 16) number. If it begins with a leading zero and has only the digits from 0 to 7, it will be considered an octal (base 8) number.

Character Class

This is the wrapper class for the primitive type **char**.

Constructors

- **Character(char value)**

This constructor makes an object that corresponds to the primitive value passed in as the parameter.

Methods

- `char charValue()`
- `boolean equals(Object obj)`
- `String toString()`

This method returns a string of length 1, where the only character in the string is the primitive **char** value represented by the **Character** object.

- `static boolean isLowerCase(char ch)`

This method returns **true** if **ch** is a lower-case character.

- `static boolean isUpperCase(char ch)`

This method returns **true** if **ch** is an upper-case character.

- `static boolean isDigit(char ch)`

This method returns **true** if **ch** is a digit.

- `static boolean isLetter(char ch)`

This method returns **true** if **ch** is a letter.

- `static boolean isLetterOrDigit(char ch)`

This method returns **true** if **ch** is a letter or a digit.

- `static char toLowerCase(char ch)`

This method returns the lower-case equivalent of **ch**. If **ch** has no lower-case equivalent, the return value will be the same as the parameter.

- `static char toUpperCase(char ch)`

This method returns the upper-case equivalent of **ch**. If **ch** has no upper-case equivalent, the return value will be the same as the parameter.

- `static int digit(char ch, int radix)`

This method returns the numeric equivalent of **ch**, in the radix (or base) specified by the second parameter.

- `static int getNumericValue(char ch)`

This method returns the numeric equivalent of **ch** as a non-negative integer.

- `static boolean isSpaceChar(char ch)`

This method returns true if **ch** is a space character, or in other words, if it is a blank.

- `static boolean isWhitespace(char ch)`

This method returns true if **ch** is a white-space character. Commonly used white-space characters include space (or blank), tab, and newline.

Class Class

The **Class** class can be used to get information about a class at runtime. Using this class, a program can find out the methods, fields (variables and constants), constructors, and superclass of a class. A program can also determine whether a particular object is a member of the class.

This class does not have any public constructors, but there are other ways of getting a **Class** object, including the static **forName** method.

The **Class** class includes two versions of some access methods. For example, there is a **getFields** method and a **getDeclaredFields** method. The method with **Declared** in its name looks only at the class itself, and will not include inherited fields in its results.

The **Object** class includes a **getClass** method. Since every object in Java inherits from **Object**, you can use the **getClass** method to get the **Class** object for any object.

The **Field**, **Method**, and **Constructor** classes are in the **java.lang.reflect** class.

Methods

- **static Class forName(String className)**
This static method takes a class or interface name as a parameter and returns the **Class** object that goes with that name.

- **Package getPackage()**

- **Class getSuperClass()**

- **Constructor[] getConstructors ()**

- **Field[] getFields ()**

- **Field[] getDeclaredFields ()**
These methods return the fields of the class represented by the **Class** object. **getFields** includes inherited fields (variables and constants) in its results, whereas **getDeclaredFields** does not.

- **Method[] getMethods ()**

- **Method[] getDeclaredMethods ()**
These methods return the methods of the class represented by the **Class** object. **getMethods** includes inherited methods (variables and constants) in its results, whereas **getDeclaredMethods** does not.

- **boolean isInstance (Object obj)**
This method returns **true** if the parameter is an instance of this class.

- **boolean isPrimitive ()**
This method tells whether this class represents a primitive type.

- **boolean isInterface ()**
This method tells whether this **Class** object represents an interface rather than a class.

- **boolean isArray ()**
This method returns **true** if this **Class** is an array.

- **Class getComponentType ()**
This method is used with an array **Class** object. It returns the component type of the array.

Example   This example shows the use of several methods in the **Class** class. It also makes use of the **getClass** method inherited from **Object**. Since the **Method** class is in **java.lang.reflect**, that package must be imported for the code to compile.

```
Class myClass;
Method[] methodList;
int[] array = new int[5];
double[] array2 = new double[5];
String str = new String("String object");

myClass = str.getClass();
methodList = myClass.getMethods();
System.out.println("Class name for str: " + myClass.getName());
System.out.println(methodList.length +
        " methods beginning with " + methodList[0].getName());

myClass = array.getClass();
System.out.println("Class name for array: " +
myClass.getName());
System.out.println("isArray: " + myClass.isArray() +
        ", component type: " + myClass.getComponentType());

myClass = array2.getClass();
System.out.println("Class name for array2: " +
myClass.getName());
System.out.println("isArray: " + myClass.isArray() +
        ", component type: " + myClass.getComponentType());
```

Output

```
Class name for str: java.lang.String
61 methods beginning with hashCode
Class name for array: [I
isArray: true, component type: int
Class name for array2: [D
isArray: true, component type: double
```

Double Class

This is the wrapper class for the primitive type **double**.

Constants

- **static final double MAX_VALUE**
- **static final double MIN_VALUE**

Constructors

- `Double(double value)`
- `Double(String s) throws NumberFormatException`

Methods

- `static String toString(double d)`
- `static Double valueOf(String s) throws NumberFormatException`
- `static double parseDouble(String s) throws NumberFormatException`
- `String toString()`
- `boolean equals(Object obj)`

Error Class

This is the parent class for various kinds of errors. Like the `Exception` class, the `Error` class inherits from `Throwable`. Unlike exceptions, however, errors should normally not be caught.

Constructors

- `Error()`
- `Error(String s)`
  The string parameter is a detail message for the error.

Example   The second `println` method call is commented out, because otherwise the compiler will flag it as an unreachable statement.

```
System.out.println("Beginning execution.");
throw new Error("This is an intentional error.");
// System.out.println("Finished executing.");
```

Output
```
Beginning execution.
Exception in thread "main" java.lang.Error: This is an intentional
error.
        at ErrorTest.main(ErrorTest.java:4)
```

Exception Class

This is the parent class for various kinds of exceptions. The methods that this class inherits from its parent class, **Throwable**, are useful for debugging programs. For instance, if you want to know where an exception is occurring in your program, you can call the `printStackTrace` method in the catch clause that handles exceptions.

Constructors

- `Exception()`
- `Exception(String s)`

Methods   Note that all of the methods here are inherited from the parent class of `Ex-ception`, which is the `Throwable` class.

- `String getMessage()`
- `String toString()`
- `void printStackTrace(PrintWriter s)`

Float Class

This is the wrapper class for the primitive type `float`.

Constants

- `static final float MAX_VALUE`
- `static final float MIN_VALUE`

Constructors

- `Float(float value)`
- `Float(double value)`
- `Float(String s) throws NumberFormatException`

Methods

- `static String toString(float f)`
- `static Float valueOf(String s) throws NumberFormatException`
- `static double parseFloat(String s) throws NumberFormatException`
- `String toString()`
- `boolean equals(Object obj)`

Integer Class

This is the wrapper class for the primitive type `int`.

Constants

- `static final int MAX_VALUE`
- `static final int MIN_VALUE`

Constructors

- `Integer(int value)`
- `Integer(String s) throws NumberFormatException`

Methods

- `static String toString(int f, int radix)`
- `static String toHexString(int i)`

- `static String toOctalString(int i)`
- `static String toBinaryString(int i)`
- `static Integer valueOf(String s) throws NumberFormatException`
- `static int parseInt(String s) throws NumberFormatException`
- `static Integer valueOf(String s, int radix)`
  `throws NumberFormatException`
- `String toString()`
- `boolean equals(Object obj)`
- `static Integer decode(String num) throws NumberFormatException`

If the string **num** begins with **0x**, **0X**, or **#**, the number will be considered a hexadecimal (base 16) number. If it begins with a leading zero and has only the digits from 0 to 7, it will be considered an octal (base 8) number.

- `int compareTo(Integer anotherInteger)`

Long Class

This is the wrapper class for the primitive type **long**.

Constants

- `static final long MAX_VALUE`
- `static final long MIN_VALUE`

Constructors

- `Long(long value)`
- `Long(String s) throws NumberFormatException`

Methods

- `static String toString(long i, int radix)`
- `static String toHexString(long i)`
- `static String toOctalString(long i)`
- `static String toBinaryString(long i)`
- `static Long valueOf(String s) throws NumberFormatException`
- `static Long valueOf(String s, int radix)`
  `throws NumberFormatException`
- `static double parseLong(String s, int radix)`
  `throws NumberFormatException`
- `String toString()`
- `boolean equals(Object obj)`
- `static Long decode(String num) throws NumberFormatException`

If the string **num** begins with **0x**, **0X**, or **#**, the number will be considered a hexadecimal (base 16) number. If it begins with a leading zero and has only the digits from 0 to 7, it will be considered an octal (base 8) number.

- `int compareTo(Long anotherLong)`

Math Class

Unlike most other classes in the Java API, this class has no constructors. All of the methods in the class are static, so there is no need to make any objects of this class.

Constants

- `static final double E`
- `static final double PI`

Methods

- `static double sin(double a)`
- `static double cos(double a)`
- `static double tan(double a)`
- `static double asin(double a)`
- `static double acos(double a)`
- `static double atan(double a)`

For trigonometric functions, angles are specified in radians. The `toRadians` and `toDegrees` methods, listed below, can be used to convert back and forth between the two units of measurements for angles. `asin` tells the arc sine, `acos` the arc cosine, and `atan` the arc tangent.

- `static double toRadians(double angdeg)`
- `static double toDegrees(double angrad)`
- `static double exp(double a)`
- `static double log(double a)`
- `static double sqrt(double a)`
- `static double ceil(double a)`
- `static double floor(double a)`
- `static double rint(double a)`
- `static double atan2(double a, double b)`
- `static double pow(double a, double b)`

This method returns the value of **a** raised to the power **b**.

- `static int round(float a)`
- `static long round(double a)`
- `static double random()`
- `static int abs(int a)`
- `static long abs(long a)`
- `static float abs(float a)`
- `static double abs(double a)`
- `static int max(int a, int b)`
- `static long max(long a, long b)`
- `static float max(float a, float b)`

- `static double max(double a, double b)`
- `static int min(int a, int b)`
- `static long min(long a, long b)`
- `static float min(float a, float b)`
- `static double min(double a, double b)`

Number Class

The **Number** class is an abstract class, which means that you cannot make **Number** objects. The class contains various methods which its subclasses implement. **BigDecimal**, **BigInteger**, **Byte**, **Double**, **Float**, **Integer**, **Long**, and **Short** are all subclasses of **Number**.

Methods

- `byte byteValue ()`
- `double doubleValue ()`
- `float floatValue ()`
- `int intValue ()`
- `long longValue ()`
- `short shortValue ()`
   Each of these methods converts the value of the object to the return type of the method. This makes it possible, for instance to convert an **Integer** object's value to the **long** type. The conversions may involve rounding or truncation.

Object Class

The **Object** class is at the top of the inheritance hierarchy in Java, so all classes inherit from it, either directly or indirectly. All objects inherit the methods of this class.

Constructors

- `Object()`

Methods

- `final Class getClass()`
   This method returns an object that represents the class of the calling object. To get the name of the class, use the **getName()** method of the class object returned by the **getClass** method.

- `int hashCode()`
- `boolean equals(Object obj)`
- `protected Object clone() throws CloneNotSupportedException`
- `String toString()`
- `final void notify()`

- `final void notifyAll()`
- `final void wait(long timeout) throws InterruptedException`
- `final void wait(long timeout, int nanos)`
  `throws InterruptedException`
- `final void wait() throws InterruptedException`
- `protected void finalize() throws Throwable`

Short Class

This is the wrapper class for the primitive type **short**.

Constants

- `static final short MAX_VALUE`
- `static final short MIN_VALUE`

Constructors

- `Short(short value)`
- `Short(String s) throws NumberFormatException`

Methods

- `static String toString(short i)`
- `static Short valueOf(String s) throws NumberFormatException`
- `static Short valueOf(String s, int radix)`
  `throws NumberFormatException`
- `static short parseShort(String s) throws NumberFormatException`
- `static short parseShort(String s, int radix)`
  `throws NumberFormatException`
- `String toString()`
- `boolean equals(Object obj)`
- `static Short decode(String num) throws NumberFormatException`
  If the string **num** begins with **0x**, **0X**, or **#**, the number will be considered a hexadecimal (base 16) number. If it begins with a leading zero and has only the digits from 0 to 7, it will be considered an octal (base 8) number.
- `int compareTo(Long anotherLong)`

String Class

The **string** class is one of the most commonly used classes in Java. It is used to represent character strings and text. Strings in Java are immutable. This is an important characteristic. Once a string is created, it cannot be changed. The methods here that appear to change a string (like **toUpperCase**, for instance) are actually returning a modified copy of the original string rather than modifying the string.

If you are working with text and need to be able to modify a string, you can use the **StringBuffer** class.

Character indexes for strings start at zero, just as array indexes do. So, for example, if you want to get the first character in a string, you would use a method call like this: **str.charAt(0)**

Constructors

- **String()**
- **String(String value)**
- **String(char[] value)**
- **String(char[] value, int offset, int count)**
- **String(byte[] bytes, int offset, int length)**
- **String(byte[] bytes)**
- **String(StringBuffer buffer)**

Methods

- **int length()**
- **char charAt(int index)**

This method returns the character at position **index** in the string. Note that the index of the first character in the string is zero.

- **void getChars(int srcBegin, int srcEnd,**
  char[] dst, int dstBegin)
- **byte[] getBytes()**
- **boolean equals(Object anObject)**
- **boolean equalsIgnoreCase(String anotherString)**
- **int compareTo(String anotherString)**
- **int compareToIgnoreCase(String str)**

If you sort strings using the standard version of **compareTo** (which does not ignore case), it will use the order of the Unicode codes for each character. Since capital *Z* has a lower code than lower-case *a*, a string beginning with lower-case *a* will come after a string beginning with upper-case *Z*. If you use the version that ignores case, all the strings beginning with *A* will come before the strings beginning with *Z*, regardless of the case of the letters.

- **boolean regionMatches(int toffset, String other,**
  int ooffset, int len)
- **boolean regionMatches(boolean ignoreCase,**
  int toffset, String other,
  int ooffset, int len)
- **boolean startsWith(String prefix, int toffset)**
- **boolean startsWith(String prefix)**
- **boolean endsWith(String suffix)**

- `int indexOf(int ch)`
- `int indexOf(int ch, int fromIndex)`
- `int lastIndexOf(int ch)`
- `int lastIndexOf(int ch, int fromIndex)`
- `int indexOf(String str)`
- `int indexOf(String str, int fromIndex)`
- `int lastIndexOf(String str)`
- `int lastIndexOf(String str, int fromIndex)`

The index methods listed here can be used to find a character or substring in a string.

- `String substring(int beginIndex)`
- `String substring(int beginIndex, int endIndex)`

This method makes a new string that includes characters starting at **beginIndex** and continuing to **endIndex −1**.

- `String concat(String str)`
- `String replace(char oldChar, char newChar)`
- `String toLowerCase()`
- `String toUpperCase()`
- `String trim()`

This method removes white space (and ASCII control characters) from both ends of the string. White space consists of spaces, tabs, and newline characters. This method returns a trimmed copy of the original string, which is not modified.

- `char[] toCharArray()`
- `static String valueOf(Object obj)`
- `static String valueOf(char[] data)`
- `static String valueOf(char[] data, int offset, int count)`

System Class

The most common use of the **System** class is to access the standard input and output streams. Note that a program cannot instantiate this class.

Variables

- `static PrintStream err`

This is an output stream used for error messages or other information that should be displayed on the screen even if the standard output stream has been redirected.

- `static InputStream in`

This stream is often used with the **BufferedReader** class to read input from the keyboard. See the description of **BufferedReader** (in the **java.io** package) for an example of using this input stream.

- `static PrintStream out`

The **print** and **println** methods of the **PrintStream** class are the most common way of printing to the screen.

Methods

- **static void exit(int status)**

This method is used to end a program. The parameter can be used to indicate error conditions.

StringBuffer Class

Unlike objects of the **String** class, objects of the **StringBuffer** class can be modified. String buffer methods are synchronized to allow use by multiple threads. Each string buffer has an initial capacity determined by the constructor used to create it. The capacity of the buffer is increased as necessary to allow for changes to the contents.

Constructors

- **StringBuffer()**
- **StringBuffer(int length)**
- **StringBuffer(String str)**

Each constructor determines the initial capacity of the string buffer in a different way. The first constructor, which has no parameters, uses a default initial capacity of 16. The second constructor takes a length parameter that tells the initial capacity. The third constructor takes a string argument that will be the initial contents of the buffer. The initial capacity of the buffer created by the third constructor will be 16 more than the length of the string parameter.

Methods

- **StringBuffer append(boolean b)**
- **StringBuffer append(char c)**
- **StringBuffer append(int i)**
- **StringBuffer append(long l)**
- **StringBuffer append(float f)**
- **StringBuffer append(double d)**

The **append** method is overloaded to allow various types of information to be added to the end of a string buffer. Values of types **boolean**, **int**, **long**, **float**, and **double** will be converted to characters before being appended to the buffer.

- **StringBuffer insert(int offset, char[] str, int index, int len)**

The first parameter tells where to insert characters in the buffer. The second parameter is an array that holds the characters to be inserted in the buffer. The third parameter tells the index of the first character in **str** that will be inserted, and the last parameter tells how many characters from the array to insert in the buffer.

- **StringBuffer insert(int offset, Object obj)**
- **StringBuffer insert(int offset, String str)**

- `StringBuffer insert(int offset, char[] str)`
- `StringBuffer insert(int offset, boolean b)`
- `StringBuffer insert(int offset, char c)`
- `StringBuffer insert(int offset, int i)`
- `StringBuffer insert(int offset, long l)`
- `StringBuffer insert(int offset, float f)`
- `StringBuffer insert(int offset, double d)`

Each of the insert methods takes an offset as a parameter. The offset determines where to insert characters in the buffer. Values of types **boolean**, **int**, **long**, **float**, and **double** will be converted to characters before being inserted in the buffer.

- `char charAt(int index)`

This method returns the character at the specified index in the buffer.

- `void setCharAt(int index, char ch)`
- `StringBuffer delete(int start, int end)`
- `StringBuffer deleteCharAt(int index)`
- `void getChars(int srcBegin, int srcEnd, char[] dst, int dstBegin)`

This method copies characters from the buffer to **dst**, starting at index **srcBegin** and ending at **srcEnd**. The fourth parameter tells where in the destination array the characters from the buffer will be stored.

- `int length()`

This method returns the length of the buffer contents. Note that the length of the buffer contents is not the same as the capacity of the buffer.

- `StringBuffer replace(int start, int end, String str)`

This method replaces characters in the buffer with characters from **str**, beginning at position **start** in the buffer and continuing to position **end** − 1.

- `void setLength(int newLength)`

This method truncates the contents of the buffer as necessary so that the new length of the contents will be **newLength**.

- `String substring(int start)`
- `String substring(int start, int end)`
- `StringBuffer reverse()`
- `String toString()`

Thread Class

This class is usually used as a parent class, rather than instantiating the **Thread** class itself. When the **start** method of a child class object is called, the Java Virtual Machine starts a new thread of execution. The first method to be executed by the new thread will be the **run** method. The Java Virtual Machine will switch back and forth between different threads in a program to give the appearance of the threads running at the same time.

Methods

- **static void sleep(long millis) throws InterruptedException**

This method causes the thread to stop executing for the specified number of milliseconds (a millisecond is a thousandth of a second).

- **void start()**

Normally a child class will not override this method. When this method is called, the Java Virtual Machine begins execution of the **run** method as a new thread of execution.

- **void run()**

Subclasses of the **Thread** class should override this method. Note that this method is **not** called directly; instead it begins execution when the **start** method of the **Thread** subclass object is called.

Throwable Class

This is the parent class for **Exception** and **Error**. Only instances of this class or its subclasses can be thrown by the **throw** statement. Throwable objects include two kinds of information, the stack trace and a text message about the error or exception. The stack trace tells which methods have begun execution but have not finished; this helps the programmer to determine which method caused the problem.

Constructors

- **Thowable()**
- **Throwable(String message)**

Methods

- **String getMessage ()**

This method gives the text message associated with the error or exception.

- **void printStackTrace ()**
- **void printStackTrace(PrintStream s)**
- **void printStackTrace(PrintWriter s)**

These methods allow the program to print the stack trace, either to the default output stream or to a specified output stream or writer.

- **StackTraceElement[] getStackTrace ()**

This method allows a program to analyze the stack trace.

java.math Package

The **java.math** package contains two big number classes, **BigInteger** and **BigDecimal**. These classes allow a program to use numbers of arbitrary precision. For example, a **BigInteger** object can represent a number that is 40 digits long. Trying to represent a 40-digit number as a regular **int** will give an "integer number too large" error. A 40-digit number can be represented as a floating-point number (float or double), but will have limited precision. For instance, adding 2 to 2.0E39 (2 times 10 to the 39th power) has no effect because of the limited precision (see the sample code and output in the **BigDecimal** class description below).

Because the standard arithmetic operators like + cannot be used with objects, the **BigInteger** and **BigDecimal** classes provide methods that implement arithmetic operations. For instance if you wanted to add 2 to the **BigInteger x**, you would use a line of code like this:

```
x.add(2);
```

The class descriptions given below list some of the more commonly used arithmetic methods that are available for use with these classes.

BigDecimal Class

This class provides a way to represent numbers of arbitrary precision that can include a fractional part. Each **BigDecimal** object has a scale value that tells how many digits are to the right of the decimal point.

BigDecimal objects are immutable, which means they cannot be changed.

Constructors

- **BigDecimal(String numberStr)**
The string parameter specifies a number that is the initial value of the object. The string can contain a sign (+ or –), and integer part, a decimal point and fraction part, and an exponent. The exponent is an **E** (upper or lower case) followed by the digits in the exponent.

- **BigDecimal(BigInteger number)**
This constructor allows a **BigInteger** value to be converted to a **BigDecimal** value.

Constants   The following constants are used to tell how a **BigDecimal** value should be rounded:

- **static int ROUND_CEILING**
This constant means that the number should be rounded toward positive infinity.

- **static int ROUND_DOWN**
This constant means that the number should be rounded toward zero.

- **static int ROUND_FLOOR**
This constant means that the number should be rounded toward negative infinity.

- **static int ROUND_HALF_DOWN**
This constant means that the number should be rounded toward the nearest integer, rounding down if two integers are equally close.

- **static int ROUND_HALF_EVEN**
This constant means that the number should be rounded toward the nearest integer, rounding to the even one if two integers are equally close.

- **static int ROUND_HALF_UP**
This constant means that the number should be rounded toward the nearest integer, rounding up if two integers are equally close.

- **static int ROUND_UNNECESSARY**

This constant asserts that the result will be exact and will not require rounding.

- **static int ROUND_UP**

This constant means that the number should be rounded away from zero.

Methods   The following methods provide basic arithmetic operations with **BigDecimal** values:

- **BigDecimal abs()**
- **BigDecimal add(BigDecimal op2)**
- **int compareTo(BigDecimal op2)**

The result of this method will be –1 if the calling object is less than **op2**, 0 if it is equal to **op2**, and 1 if it is greater than **op2**.

- **BigDecimal divide(BigDecimal op2, int round)**
- **boolean equals(Object op2)**
- **BigDecimal max(BigDecimal op2)**
- **BigDecimal min(BigDecimal op2)**
- **BigDecimal multiply(BigDecimal op2)**
- **BigDecimal negate()**
- **BigDecimal subtract(BigDecimal op2)**

These methods convert **BigDecimal** values to other types:

- **double doubleValue()**
- **float floatValue()**
- **int intValue()**
- **long longValue()**
- **BigInteger toBigInteger()**

The methods shown below are used to get or change the scale of the **BigDecimal**:

- **BigDecimal movePointLeft(int places)**
- **BigDecimal movePointRight(int places)**

The parameter for each of these methods specifies how many places to the right or left to move the decimal point.

- **int scale()**

This method returns the scale of the **BigDecimal**, which tells how many digits are to the right of the decimal point.

- **BigDecimal setScale(int scale)**
- **BigDecimal setScale(int scale, int round)**

Example   The following code demonstrates the use of **BigDecimal** values and compares their use to the use of **double** values. The **add** and **multiply** methods are used instead of addition and multiplication operators.

```
BigDecimal x, y, z, w;
double xDouble;
x = new
BigDecimal("1000000000000000000000000000000000000000");
y = new BigDecimal("2");
w = new BigDecimal("2.005");

System.out.println("A BigDecimal x: " + x);
z = x.multiply(y);
System.out.println("x multiplied by 2: " + z);
z = z.add(w);
System.out.println("x times 2 plus 2.005: " + z);
System.out.println("Scale: " + z.scale());
xDouble = 1000000000000000000000000000000000000000.0;
System.out.println("xDouble of type double: " + xDouble
        + "\nxDouble times 2: " + (xDouble * 2.0)
        + "\nxDouble times 2 plus 2.005: " +
        (xDouble * 2.0 + 2.005));
```

The preceding lines of code give the following output. Not that when 2.005 is added to the **BigDecimal**, it shows in the result. However, when 2.005 is added to the **double** variable, it does note show in the result because of the limited precision of the **double** type. Also not that the final **BigDecimal** value has three values to the right of the decimal point, and so has a scale of three.

```
A BigDecimal x: 1000000000000000000000000000000000000000
x multiplied by 2: 2000000000000000000000000000000000000000
x times 2 plus 2.005:
2000000000000000000000000000000000000002.005
Scale: 3
xDouble of type double: 1.0E39
xDouble times 2: 2.0E39
xDouble times 2 plus 2.005: 2.0E39
```

BigInteger Class

This class provides a way to represent integers of arbitrary precision. **BigInteger** objects are immutable, which means they cannot be changed.

Constructors

- **BigInteger(String numberStr)**
The string parameter specifies a number that is the initial value of the object. The string can have a minus sign at the beginning but otherwise can only contain decimal digits.

Constants   The **BigInteger** class provides the following two constants:

- **static final BigInteger ZERO**
- **static final BigInteger ONE**

Methods   The following methods provide basic arithmetic operations with `BigInteger` values:

- `BigInteger abs()`
- `BigInteger add(BigInteger op2)`
- `int compareTo(BigInteger op2)`

The result of this method will be –1 if the calling object is less than `op2`, 0 if it is equal to `op2`, and 1 if it is greater than `op2`.

- `BigInteger divide(BigInteger op2, int round)`
- `boolean equals(Object op2)`
- `BigInteger gcd(BigInteger op2)`

This method returns the greatest common denominator (GCD) of the calling object and **op2**.

- `BigInteger max(BigInteger op2)`
- `BigInteger min(BigInteger op2)`
- `BigInteger mod(BigInteger op2)`
- `BigInteger multiply(BigInteger op2)`
- `BigInteger negate()`
- `BigInteger pow(BigInteger op2)`
- `BigInteger remainder(BigInteger op2)`

This method returns the remainder when the calling object is divided by **op2**.

- `BigInteger subtract(BigInteger op2)`

These methods convert `BigInteger` values to other types:

- `double doubleValue()`
- `float floatValue()`
- `int intValue()`
- `long longValue()`

Example   The following code demonstrates the use of `BigInteger`. The `multiply` method is used instead of the multiplication operator.

```
BigInteger x, y, z;
x = new BigInteger("20000000000000000000000000000000");
y = new BigInteger("300000000000000000");
z = x.multiply(y);
System.out.print("x: " + x + "\ny: " + y + "\nz: " + z + "\n");
```

The preceding lines of code give the following output:

```
x: 20000000000000000000000000000000
y: 300000000000000000
z: 6000000000000000000000000000000000000000000000000
```

java.net Package

The **java.net** package is used for network communication between Java programs. This package provides socket classes that can be used to allow network communication between a server program and a client program. The server program creates a server socket, and then accepts connections from clients. Each client program must have the address (full host name and port number) of the server program in order to connect with the server. The sample code in this section includes an example of the typical use of a server socket and of sockets in a client.

HttpURLConnection Class

This is a child class of the abstract class **URLConnection**. Whereas the **URLConnection** class provides support for URL connections in general, this class provides support specifically for the HTTP protocol (HyperText Transport Protocol).

Constants

- **static final int HTTP_NOT_FOUND**
- **static final int HTTP_OK**
These constants, along with others (not listed here because they are too numerous), are returned by the **getResponseCode** method.

Methods

- **int getResponseCode() throws IOException**
This method extracts a response code number from the response message and returns it as an **int** value. The constants **HTTP_NOT_FOUND** and **HTTP_OK** are two possible values for the return value of this method.
- **String getResponseMessage() throws IOException**
Examples of the return value of this method are **"OK"** or **"Not Found."**
- **void setRequestMethod(String method) throws ProtocolException**
The two most commonly used request methods are **GET** and **POST**.

InetAddress Class

This class is used to represent IP (Internet Protocol) addresses. An **InetAddress** can be used to specify the host when creating a new **Socket** object.

Methods

- **static InetAddress getByName(String host) throws UnknownHostException**
This static method can be used to get an **InetAddress** by specifying either a name (like **"java.sun.com"**) or a number (like **"192.18.97.71"**). One use for the return value of this method is to pass it as a parameter to a constructor of the **Socket** class.

ServerSocket Class

There are three basic steps to using the **ServerSocket** class

1. Create a server socket that will "listen" on a specified port. A port is a number that helps the operating system keep track of the programs using network communication. The port number must be available to the client programs. When writing client-server systems, you will want to choose port numbers that are not used for other purposes. On UNIX systems, port numbers should be between 1000 and 64000

2. Call the **accept** method to accept connections from client programs. The accept method will either return a new socket or will time out (if a time-out period has been set).

3. Use the socket returned by the **accept** method call to communicate with clients.

Remember that firewalls and other network security mechanisms can prevent network communication.

Constructors

- **ServerSocket(int port) throws IOException**

Methods

- **Socket accept() throws IOException**
The server program calls this method when it is ready to communicate with a client. The method does not return until a client connects to the server's host address and port number or the time-out period for the socket has passed. The return value is a socket that can be used to communicate with the client. The server uses the output stream of the socket to write to the client and the input stream of the socket to read from the client.

- **int getSoTimeout() throws IOException**

- **void setSoTimeout(int timeout) throws SocketException**
These two methods are used to get and set the time-out period of the socket. If the time-out period is set to zero, then a call to the **accept** method will block until a client connects. If the time-out period is set to a value greater than zero, then a call to **accept** will return when a client connects or **timeout** milliseconds have passed, whichever comes first.

- **void close() throws IOException**

Example The following code example illustrates a simple server program that can work in conjunction with the **Client** example shown in the description of the **Socket** class.

```
import java.net.*;
import java.io.*;
```

```
class Server {
    public static void main(String[] args) {
        ServerSocket serverSock = null;
            Socket sock = null;
            int port = 55555;
        BufferedReader in = null;
        BufferedWriter out = null;

        try {
            serverSock = new ServerSocket(port);

            sock = serverSock.accept();
            in = new BufferedReader(
                    new InputStreamReader(
                        sock.getInputStream()));
            out = new BufferedWriter(
                    new OutputStreamWriter(

            sock.getOutputStream()));

            out.write("Hello from the server!\n");

            out.close();
            in.close();
            sock.close();
            serverSock.close();

        } catch (IOException e) {
            e.printStackTrace();
        }
    }
}
```

Socket Class

This class is used to communicate over the Internet. It is used on the client side. A different class, **ServerSocket**, is used on the server side. The descriptions for this class and the **ServerSocket** class include sample code showing how to set up client-server communication.

Constructors
- **Socket(InetAddress address, int port)**
- **Socket(String host, int port)**

Methods
- **InputStream getInputStream()**

- **OutputStream getOutputStream()**

These two methods provide access to the input and output streams of the socket. These streams can be used with readers and writers, as illustrated in the sample code that follows.

- **void close()**

Example   The following code shows how to open a client socket that can be used to communicate with a server. Methods of the **BufferedReader** class can be used with **in** to read information from the server, and methods of the **BufferedWriter** class can be used with **out** to write information to the server.

```java
import java.io.*;
import java.net.*;

public class Client {
    public static void main(String[] args) {
    Socket mySocket;
    BufferedReader in = null;
    BufferedWriter out = null;
    String hostName = "myhost.mydomain.edu";
    int port = 55555;
    String fromServer = null;
    try {
    mySocket = new Socket(hostName, port);
    in = new BufferedReader(new InputStreamReader(

mySocket.getInputStream()));
            out = new BufferedWriter(new OutputStreamWriter(

mySocket.getOutputStream()));

            fromServer = in.readLine();
            System.out.println("read from server: " + fromServer);

        } catch (UnknownHostException e) {
            System.err.println("unknown host: " + hostName);
        } catch (IOException e) {
            System.err.println(
                "Couldn't connect to: "
                + hostName + " port: " + port);
        }
    }
}
```

URL Class

A URL is a Uniform Resource Locator, sometimes known as a "Web address." Here is an example of a URL:

http://java.sun.com/docs/books/tutorial/index.html

The main parts of a URL are a protocol, a host computer name, and a path. In this example the protocol is **http**, which stands for HyperText Transfer Protocol. The next part of the URL is the host computer name, which in this case is **java.sun.com**. The last part, **docs/books/tutorial/index.html,** is the path. The path tells what information should be retrieved from the host computer.

You can use URL objects in Java programs to read files from other computers on the Internet. First create a URL object with the correct information, and then use the **openConnection** method to get a connection for that URL. Once you have the connection you can use the input stream of the connection to read a file. In some cases you can also write to a URL.

Note that the **getDocumentBase** and **getCodeBase** methods of the **Applet** class return **URL** objects as their return values.

Constructors

- **URL(String stringURL) throws MalformedURLException**

The parameter for this constructor is a URL in string form, which is the way you type a URL in for a Web browser.

- **URL(String protocol, String host, String path)**
  throws MalformedURLException

The protocol, host, and path can be specified separately with this constructor.

- **URL(URL context, String spec) throws MalformedURLException**

The context parameter can be the URL returned by the **getDocumentBase** or **getCodeBase** methods of the **Applet** class.

Methods

- **URLConnection openConnection()**

This method returns a **URLConnection** for the URL. The declared type of the returned value is **URLconnection**, but in many cases the actual type returned will be a child class of **URLConnection**, such as **HttpURLConnection**.

- **InputStream openStream() throws IOException**

URLConnection Class

This is an abstract class, so no objects of it are actually created. However, variables of this type can be used to refer to objects of child classes, such as **HttpURLConnection**.

Methods

- **boolean getDoInput()**
- **void setDoInput(boolean doInput)**

Get and set the flag that tells whether the connection will be used for input. A **true** value means that the program will be reading from the URL associated with the connection. If the **doOutput** flag has not been set, the default value for the **doInput** flag is true. If the **doOutput** flag has been set to **true**, the default value for the **doInput** flag is **false**.

- **`boolean getDoOutput()`**
- **`void setDoOutput(boolean doOutput)`**

Get and set the flag that tells whether the connection will be used for output. A **true** value means that the program will be writing to the URL associated with the connection. The default is **false**.

- **`InputStream getInputStream() throws IOException`**
- **`OutputStream getOutputStream() throws IOException`**

The **InputStream** and **OutputStream** can be used with classes and methods from the java.io package to read from the URL and write to it.

- **`String getRequestProperty(String key)`**
- **`void setRequestProperty(String key, String value)`**

These two methods get and set request properties, such as **Content-Type** and **Content-Length**. For writing URL-encoded text to a URL, you would use a method call like this one:

```
conn.setRequestProperty ("Content-Type",
                         "application/x-www-form-urlencoded");
```

For writing normal (unencoded) text you could use a method call like this one:

```
conn.setRequestProperty("Content-type", "text/plain");
```

The actual keys (property names) and property values used depend on the type of connection. **Content-Type** and **Content-Length** are two properties used with HTTP connections.

URLDecoder Class

This class provides a method that will take a string in the URL-encoded format and return a decoded string. Since the only method in this class (other than inherited methods) is a static method, the constructor for this class is not often used. See the description for the **URLEncoder** class for a description of URL encoding.

Methods

- **`static String decode(String s)`**

This static method takes a URL-encoded string and returns the decoded string. It is a very useful method if you want to write a Java program that receives information from an HTML form.

URLEncoder Class

This class provides a method that will put strings into the format used to include text as part of a URL. Since the only method in this class (other than inherited methods) is a static method, the constructor for this class is not often used.

Encoding does not change the letters (A–Z, upper and lower case), the digits (0–9), or the characters '.', '-', '*', or '_'. All space characters are replaced with the plus sign '+'. All other characters are replaced with a percent sign '%' followed by two hexadecimal digits which are the lower eight bits of the character code.

Methods

- **static String encode(String s)**

This static method takes a URL-encoded string and returns the decoded string. The URL-encoded format is used with HTML forms that pass information to CGI scripts, so you can use the **encode** method to send information to a CGI script from a Java program.

java.text Package

The **java.text** package includes classes that are useful for formatting and parsing text, including numbers, dates, and times. The descriptions included here focus on formatting rather than parsing.

DateFormat Class

This class provides static methods that return an object used to format dates and times. The kind of formatting object returned depends on the method used and the parameters to the method. The formatting object can be for the date, for the time, or both.

This description focuses on formatting dates and times, but the **DateFormat** class can also be used to parse date and time strings.

Constants

- **static final int FULL**
- **static final int LONG**
- **static final int MEDIUM**
- **static final int SHORT**
- **static final int DEFAULT**

These constants are used to specify the style of the date and/or time. **FULL** is the most complete and does not abbreviate anything. **SHORT** uses only numbers for the date, like **4/27/03** instead of **April 27, 2003**. The value of **DEFAULT** is **MEDIUM**.

The following constants are used to specify fields in the date or time. They are all declared as **public static final int** values. The following fields are used with dates:

ERA_FIELD	YEAR_FIELD
DATE_FIELD	MONTH_FIELD
DAY_OF_WEEK_FIELD	DAY_OF_YEAR_FIELD
WEEK_OF_YEAR_FIELD	WEEK_OF_MONTH_FIELD
DAY_OF_WEEK_IN_MONTH_FIELD	

These fields are used with the time:

HOUR_OF_DAY1_FIELD	HOUR_OF_DAY0_FIELD
MINUTE_FIELD	SECOND_FIELD
MILLISECOND_FIELD	TIMEZONE_FIELD

HOUR_OF_DAY1_FIELD is a one-based value where the first hour is numbered 1. **HOUR_OF_DAY0_FIELD** is a zero-based value where the first hour is numbered zero.

Constructors Rather than use constructors in the usual way, you can get instances of the **DateFormat** class by using the **GetTimeInstance**, **GetDateInstance**, and **GetDateTimeInstance** static methods.

Methods There are several static methods for obtaining date formatting objects. The style parameter for these methods should be **SHORT**, **MEDIUM**, **LONG**, **FULL**, or **DEFAULT**. These methods all use the default locale. There are additional versions of these methods that have a locale parameter. The **getInstance** method uses the **SHORT** style for time and for date.

- `static final DateFormat getInstance()`
- `static final DateFormat getDateInstance()`
- `static final DateFormat getDateInstance(int style)`
- `static final DateFormat getDateTimeInstance()`
- `static final DateFormat getDateTimeInstance(int dateStyle, int timeStyle)`
- `static final DateFormat getTimeInstance()`
- `static final DateFormat getTimeInstance(int style)`
- `final String format(Date date)`

This method returns a string containing the complete formatted date, in the style specified by the method used to get the instance.

- `abstract StringBuffer format(Date date, StringBuffer strBuff, FieldPosition fieldPos)`

This method appends the formatted date and/or time string to **strBuff**, and also returns a reference to a string buffer that contains the formatted date/time string. The value of **fieldPos** passed in specifies a field in the date/time string, and the output value of the **fieldPos** parameter contains the beginning and ending indexes of the specified field.

Example Here is an example of using the **DateFormat** class:

```
Date theDate = new Date();
DateFormat theFormat;
theFormat = DateFormat.getDateTimeInstance(DateFormat.FULL,

DateFormat.SHORT);
System.out.println("date: " + theFormat.format(theDate));
```

Output:

```
date: Saturday, April 28, 2001 3:51 PM
```

Note that **getDateTimeInstance** takes two parameters, one that tells the style for the date, and the second to tell the style of the time. If the style of the time had been **FULL**, it would have printed out the seconds and the time zone as well as the hours, minutes, and AM/PM.

You can see an example of using the **FieldPosition** class with the **DateFormat** class in the section that describes the **FieldPosition** class.

DecimalFormat Class

DecimalFormat is used to format integers, fixed-point numbers, scientific notation, percentages, and currency amounts. As with the **NumberFormat** class, this class can be used to parse numbers in addition to formatting them, but the description here focuses on formatting.

There are two ways to define the format of a number: using patterns, and using method calls that set various characteristics of the format. Applying a pattern will override values previously set using method calls, and setting values with method calls will override values previously set by a pattern.

The characteristics of a format include the minimum and maximum number of integer digits, the minimum and maximum number of fraction digits, and the grouping size. The grouping size is the number of integer digits that are grouped with commas.

The table below shows some of the characters that have special meaning in a pattern, along with their meaning.

0	digit
#	digit, or blank if the digit would be a leading or trailing zero
.	decimal separator
,	grouping separator

The **0** character is used to show the minimum number of digits in the formatted number. A **0** cannot appear before a **#** in the integer part of the pattern or after a **#** in the fraction part of the pattern. For example, the pattern **"0##"** is not a valid pattern.

The **#** sign will show as a digit if the digit is nonzero and is not a leading or trailing zero. A leading zero is a zero in the integer part of the number where all the digits to the left of it are zero. A trailing zero is a zero in the fraction part of the number where all the digits to the right of it are zero.

See the code example at the end of this section for examples of patterns and the corresponding formatted output.

Constants

- **static final int FRACTION_FIELD**
- **static final int INTEGER_FIELD**

Constructors

- **DecimalFormat()**
- **DecimalFormat(String pattern)**

Methods

- **void applyPattern(String pattern)**
This method specifies a pattern to use in formatting numbers. See the code example below for an example of this method's use and for two examples of patterns.

- **void setGroupingSize(int newValue)**
This method sets the number of digits that will separated by commas (or the character defined as the grouping separator for the current locale).

- `void setMaximumIntegerDigits(int newValue)`
- `void setMinimumIntegerDigits(int newValue)`
- `void setMaximumFractionDigits(int newValue)`
- `void setMinimumFractionDigits(int newValue)`

Setting the minimum number of digits determines how many leading zeros (for the integer part of the number) or trailing zeros (for the fraction part) will be printed. Setting the maximum number of digits determines whether or not the number will be truncated.

- `String getPositivePrefix()`
- `void setPositivePrefix(String newValue)`
- `String getNegativePrefix()`
- `void setNegativePrefix(String newValue)`
- `String getPositiveSuffix()`
- `void setPositiveSuffix(String newValue)`
- `String getNegativeSuffix()`
- `void setNegativeSuffix(String newValue)`

Prefixes and suffixes can be used to include currency symbols, percent signs, and various ways of indicating a negative number (minus sign or parentheses).

The following two methods are inherited from **NumberFormat**:

- `final String format(double number)`
- `final String format(long number)`

Example   In the following code example, a **DecimalFormat** object is used to format several numbers. The first pattern used, **"00"**, means to print at least two digits for the formatted number. Without formatting, printing 3 for the hours and 9 for the minutes would print as **3:9**, which is not the correct format for a time of day. Using the pattern makes the minutes value print as two digits, giving the correctly formatted time of **3:09**.

The second part of the example shows how to use a pattern to set the grouping size. The number of digits between commas is called the grouping size. If a different locale were used, the same pattern could have formatted the number with a comma for the decimal separator and periods for the grouping separator (to separate the powers of 10). Note that even though there is only one comma in the pattern, the formatter added more than one comma to separate the powers of 10.

```
DecimalFormat dFmt = new DecimalFormat("00");
System.out.println("the time is " + 3 + ":" + dFmt.format(9));
dFmt.applyPattern("#,###.##");
System.out.println("a long number " +
                    dFmt.format(123456789.4));
```

Output:

```
the time is 3:09
a long number 123,456,789.40
```

FieldPosition Class

This class is used with descendants of the `Format` class to hold information about a field. A field position provides both input information for a method and output information. The output information is the beginning and ending index of the field in the formatted string. The input information is the field of interest.

For example, with a `DateFormat` object, a `FieldPosition` object might have the value `DateFormat.MONTH_FIELD`, which indicates that the formatting method will record the beginning and ending index of the month as the output information. The following lines of code show a short example:

```
fieldPos = new FieldPosition(DateFormat.MONTH_FIELD);
theFormat.format(theDate, strBuff, fieldPos);
System.out.println("month: " +
strBuff.substring(fieldPos.getBeginIndex(),
fieldPos.getEndIndex()));
```

The date format in this case was long, so the month printed out is the text name of the month, like this:

```
month: April
```

Constructors

- `FieldPosition(int field)`

The `field` parameter is a constant defined in one of the format classes.

Methods

- `int getBeginIndex()`
- `int getEndIndex()`

These methods can be used with the substring method of the `StringBuffer` class to retrieve a field from the string buffer, as shown in the example above.

NumberFormat Class

This class inherits from `NumberFormat`, which in turn inherits from the abstract class `Format`. `NumberFormat` is an abstract class, so it cannot be instantiated. Instead it can be used to get instances of child classes, and they do the actual formatting.

Constructors Rather than use constructors in the usual way, you can get instances of a number-formatting class by using the static methods `getInstance`, `getCurrencyInstance`, `getPercentInstance`, and `getNumberInstance`.

Methods There are several static methods used for obtaining number-formatting objects. Each of these methods returns a reference to an instance of a child class of `NumberFormat`, such as `DecimalFormat`.

- `static final NumberFormat getInstance()`
- `static final NumberFormat getCurrencyInstance()`
- `static final NumberFormat getPercentInstance()`

- `static final NumberFormat getNumberInstance(int style)`

Each of these methods also has a version that accepts a locale as a parameter.

The following example illustrates the use of a static method to obtain a reference to a **NumberFormat** object. The currency symbol used depends on the locale in use. Note that there are two digits to the right of the decimal point in the formatted number.

```
NumberFormat fmt = NumberFormat.getCurrencyInstance();
System.out.println("the amount is " + fmt.format(5.7));
```

Output:

```
the amount is $5.70
```

java.util Package

This package contains utility classes that can be used in a wide variety of programs. An important part of this package is the group of classes and interfaces used to work with collections, such as vectors or lists. The descriptions for all of the collections classes and interfaces are in a separate section that follows this one.

Calendar Class

The **Calendar** class is used to calculate various units of time, including months, days, years, hours, minutes, and seconds. It can also calculate the day of the week, the week of the month, and other values.

A typical way to use a **Calendar** object is to set the time, and then use the **get** method with a field number constant (such as **DAY_OF_WEEK**) to get a value. You can also perform calendar arithmetic, such as adding 30 days to a date.

Constants   All of the following constants are **static int** values.

Field numbers:

AM_PM	DAY_OF_MONTH	DAY_OF_WEEK
DAY_OF_WEEK_IN_MONTH	DAY_OF_YEAR	DST_OFFSET
ERA	HOUR	HOUR_OF_DAY
MILLISECOND	MINUTE	MONTH
SECOND	WEEK_OF_MONTH	WEEK_OF_YEAR
YEAR	ZONE_OFFSET	

Values for the **AM_PM** field:

AM	PM

Values for the **DAY_OF_WEEK** field:

SUNDAY	MONDAY	TUESDAY
WEDNESDAY	THURSDAY	FRIDAY
SATURDAY		

Values for the **MONTH** field:

JANUARY	FEBRUARY	MARCH
APRIL	MAY	JUNE
JULY	AUGUST	SEPTEMBER
OCTOBER	NOVEMBER	DECEMBER

Constructors

- `Calendar()`

This constructor produces a `Calendar` object with the default time zone and locale.

- `Calendar(TimeZone zone, Locale locale)`

This constructor allows you to specify the time zone and locale of the calendar. The locale object gives information about the country and/or the language of the calendar.

Methods   The methods below are used to get and set the time in a **Calendar** object. Note that the time in this case includes both the date (year, month and day) and the time (hours, minutes, seconds, and fractions of seconds).

- `Date getTime()`
- `void setTime(Date date)`
- `void set(int year, int month, int date)`
- `void set(int year, int month, int date, int hour, int minute)`
- `static Calendar getInstance()`

This static method returns a `Calendar` object that has its time set to the current date and time (based on the default time zone and locale).

These methods are access methods used to get and set the calendar's fields, such as the month or the day of the week:

- `int get(int field)`
- `void set(int field, int value)`

The `field` value is specified by using one of the constants described earlier, such as **MONTH** or **DAY_OF_WEEK**.

The following methods perform calendar arithmetic:

- `void add(int field, int amount)`

Adds a signed amount to the specified field. Higher-level fields will be changed as necessary. For example, if two months are added to a date in December, the month field will change to **FEBRUARY** and one will be added to the year field also. The amount added can be negative.

- `void roll(int field, int amount)`

This method adds the amount to the field without affecting higher-level fields. For example, if two months are added to a date in December, the month field will change to **FEBRUARY** but the year field will not change. The amount added can be negative.

A subclass of `Calendar` called `GregorianCalendar` provides a `roll` method that gives better results in some situations.

The **before** and **after** methods are used to compare dates and/or times.

- `boolean after(Object date)`
- `boolean before(Object date)`

Example   In this code, the **getInstance** static method is used to get a `Calendar` object with the current time. When the calendar is rolled 24 hours, the day of the week does not change. However, when 24 hours are added, the day of the week changes.

```
Calendar myCal;
myCal = Calendar.getInstance();

System.out.println("Day of week: " +
            myCal.get(Calendar.DAY_OF_WEEK));

myCal.roll(Calendar.HOUR, 24);
System.out.println("Day of week after roll: "
            + myCal.get(Calendar.DAY_OF_WEEK));

myCal.add(Calendar.HOUR, 24);
System.out.println("Day of week after add: "
            + myCal.get(Calendar.DAY_OF_WEEK));
```

Output

```
Day of week: 5
Day of week after roll: 5
Day of week after add: 6
```

Date Class

Date objects are used to keep track of both date (year, month, and day) and time (hours, minutes, seconds, and fractions of seconds). The constructor of the **Date** class provides a way to get the current date (and time). Methods in the **Date** class provide the means to compare dates.

To put the date in string format, use the **DateFormat** class. To get the components of the date (year, month, hour, etc.) use the **Calendar** class.

Constructors

- **Date()**

This constructor initializes the date object to contain the current time. Note that the time includes year, month, and day of the month as well as hours, minutes, and seconds.

Methods

- **boolean after(Date date2)**

This method returns **true** if the calling object's date comes after the parameter date (**date2**).

- **boolean before(Date date2)**

This method returns **true** if the calling object's date comes before the parameter date (**date2**).

Locale Class

Some of the information used in Java programs depends on the country or the language being used. For example, the currency sign displayed by a program should be the correct one for the country where the program is used. You can use the **Locale** class to specify the country and language in which a program is running, and classes such as **NumberFormat** will use the information to correctly format data.

Constants   Constants for countries:

CANADA	CANADA_FRENCH	JAPAN	CHINA	FRANCE
GERMANY	ITALY	US	KOREA	PRC
TAIWAN	UK			

Constants for languages:

CHINESE	ENGLISH	FRENCH	GERMAN	ITALIAN
JAPANESE	KOREAN			

Constructors

- `Locale(String language)`
- `Locale(String language, String country)`

The language codes are the lower-case, two-letter ISO-639 codes, and the country codes are the upper-case, two-letter ISO-3166 codes. These codes can be found on various Web sites.

Methods

- `boolean equals(Object obj)`

This method determines whether the **obj** locale is equal to another locale.

- `String getCountry()`
- `String getDisplayCountry()`
- `String getLanguage()`
- `String getDisplayLanguage()`

The display versions of these methods return a string that is suitable for display to the user. The information returned by the other methods is an abbreviation that may not be clear to some users. There is another version of each of these methods that takes a locale as a parameter and returns the information in the correct format for that locale.

- `static Locale[] getAvailableLocales()`

This method returns a list of all the installed locales.

- `static void setDefault(Locale loc)`

This method sets the default locale for the Java Virtual Machine.

Random Class

This class can be used to generate pseudorandom numbers. In some situations it is useful to be able to repeat a sequence of numbers. For instance, in testing a game you might want to use the same sequence of numbers before and after fixing a bug. You can repeat a sequence of numbers by using the same seed at the beginning and by repeating the same sequence of method calls to the **Random** object. The seed is a number used to initialize the random number generator. The current time of day is often used as a seed.

Constructors

- **Random()**

This constructor uses the current time (in milliseconds) as a seed to initialize the random number generator.

- **Random(long seed)**

This constructor uses its parameter to initialize the random number generator. Using the same seed and the same sequence of method calls will give the same sequence of random numbers.

Methods   Most of the methods in the **Random** class are used to get a random number. Different methods return different types of values, so use the one that gives the type of value that you want.

- **boolean nextBoolean()**
- **double nextDouble()**
- **float nextFloat()**
- **int nextInt()**
- **long nextLong()**

Each of the preceding methods is used to generate uniformly distributed numbers of the type in the method name. The methods that return floating-point values (**nextDouble** and **nextFloat**) return values between 0.0 and 1.0. The methods that return integer values will sometimes return negative numbers.

- **int nextInt(int n)**

This method returns uniformly distributed integer values, in the range from zero to less than **n**.

- **double nextGaussian()**

This method returns numbers with a Gaussian ("normal") distribution.

- **void setSeed(long seed)**

This method changes the seed of the random number generator, and this in turn changes the sequence of numbers that will be generated.

The **random** method in the **Math** class can be used to generate random double values in the range of 0.0 to 1.0 without explicitly creating a **Random** object.

Example   In this code, 1 is added to the result of **nextInt**, so that the minimum value will be 1 and the maximum value will be 6.

```
Random roller;
int dieRoll;

roller = new Random();
System.out.print("Five die rolls:");
for (int i = 0; i <5; i++) {
    dieRoll = roller.nextInt(6) + 1;
    System.out.print(" " + dieRoll);
}
System.out.println();
```

Output
```
Five die rolls: 3 5 1 6 2
```

Scanner Class

The **Scanner** class provides an easy way to get input from the keyboard or a file. It can also be used to parse strings. A parameter to the constructor specifies the source of the input, such as **System.in** or a file. Then methods such as **nextInt** or **nextDouble** can be used to read and parse values of different types. There are also methods for determining whether an input item of a particular type is available. These methods have names like **hasNextInt** or **hasNextDouble**.

The **Scanner** class has some pattern-matching methods (such as **findInLine**) that are beyond the scope of this book but are described in the Java API documentation. Specification of delimiters (other than the default white space delimiters) is possible, but is also beyond the scope of this book.

Constructors

- **Scanner(InputStream source)**
If **System.in** is passed as a parameter to this constructor, the scanner can be used to get input from the keyboard.

- **Scanner(File source) throws FileNotFoundException**
If **new File("data.txt")** is passed as a parameter to this constructor, the scanner will read from the file **data.txt**. If **data.txt** (or whatever file is specified) does not exist, a **FileNotFoundException** will occur.

- **Scanner(String source)**
When a string is passed as a parameter to the constructor, the scanner will use characters from the string instead of reading from the keyboard or a file.

Methods

- **boolean hasNext()**
- **boolean hasNextBigDecimal()**
- **boolean hasNextBigInteger()**
- **boolean hasNextBoolean()**
- **boolean hasNextByte()**
- **boolean hasNextDouble()**
- **boolean hasNextFloat()**
- **boolean hasNextInt()**
- **boolean hasNextLine()**
- **boolean hasNextLong()**
- **boolean hasNextShort()**

The preceding methods determine whether the scanner has an item of the indicated type. The scanner does not advance past any input when one of these methods is called. In other words, calling one of these methods does not affect the state of the input source. These methods might block (wait for input) if no input is available.

- `String next()`
- `BigDecimal nextBigDecimal()`
- `BigInteger nextBigInteger()`
- `boolean nextBoolean()`
- `byte nextByte()`
- `double nextDouble()`
- `float nextFloat()`
- `int nextInt()`
- `String nextLine()`
- `long nextLong()`
- `short nextShort()`

The preceding methods find and return an item, and then advance past the item. If the next input item is the wrong type, an **InputMismatchException** will occur. These methods might block (wait for input) if no input is available.

The string returned by **nextLine** does not include the line separator character(s).

- `close()`

This method closes the scanner.

Example

This program will keep reading **int** values from the keyboard until the user types something that is not an **int**. Notice that the prompt to type a number is printed before **hasNextInt** is called. Otherwise, **hasNextInt** would block (wait) until the user entered a value. In that case the prompt wouldn't be printed and the user wouldn't know what to type.

```java
import java.util.Scanner;

public class Scan {
    public static void main(String[] args) {
        Scanner scan = new Scanner(System.in);
        int i = 1;

        System.out.print("Type a number: ");
        while (scan.hasNextInt()) {
            i = scan.nextInt();
            System.out.println("The number is: " + i);
            System.out.print("Type a number: ");
        }
        System.out.println("Finished.");
    }
}
```

Executing the preceding code gives this output:

```
Type a number: 42
The number is: 42
Type a number: 38
The number is: 38
Type a number: a
Finished.
```

Passing the parameter "**42 38 a**" to the **Scanner** constructor will produce the same results as the preceding output (except that the numbers and newline characters typed by the user will not show on the screen).

StringTokenizer Class

Tokens in a string can be words, lines, or any other part of a string separated from the other parts of the string by a delimiter. For instance, if a space character were used as the delimiter in a string, the tokens would be words and the **StringTokenizer** class could be used to get the words from the string in order.

The **PageWriter** example demonstrates the use of the **StringTokenizer** class, using the following lines:

```
StringTokenizer parser = new StringTokenizer(pageInfo, ";");
String lastName = parser.nextToken();
String firstName = parser.nextToken();
```

The first line creates the tokenizer objects and sets the delimiter to be the semicolon character. Each of the next two lines gets a token from the string.

Constructors

- **StringTokenizer(String str)**
This constructor takes the string which will be tokenized as its only parameter. In this case it uses the default delimiters, which are the white-space characters of space, tab, newline, carriage-return, and linefeed characters. Delimiter characters are not returned as part of the token.

- **StringTokenizer(String str, String delim)**
This constructor takes the string to tokenize and a second string parameter which contains the delimiter characters. Delimiter characters are not returned as part of the token.

- **StringTokenizer(String str, String delim, boolean returnDelims)**
The first two parameters for this constructor are the same as for the two preceding constructors. The third parameter tells whether delimiters should be returned with the tokens.

Methods

- **boolean hasMoreTokens()**
This method tells whether there are more tokens in the string.

- **String nextToken()**
This method returns the next token from the string.

- **String nextToken(String delim)**
This method changes the delimiters for the tokenizer and then returns the next token.

- **int countTokens()**
This method tells how many more tokens are left in the string.

java.util Package: Collections Framework

This section describes the classes and interfaces that are part of the Java collections framework.

Many classes and interfaces in the collections framework make use of generics, a concept that first appeared in Java in version 1.5. Generic classes and interfaces have type parameters specified in angle brackets, **<** and **>**. For instance, you could make a vector of strings by using a statement like this.

```
Vector<String> v = new Vector<String>();
```

In this case, **v** can only have **String** objects (or objects of classes descended from **String**) added to it. Attempting to add any other type of object will result in a compiler error.

Some type parameters are wild-card parameters, indicated by a question mark. For example, the **containsAll** method of the **Collection<E>** interface takes a parameter of type **Collection<?>**. This means that the objects in the collection can be any class. The elements of the collection must be instances of a single class (or descendant classes).

Sometimes a wild-card parameter will be more restrictive and specify that the class can be any descendant of a given class. The **addAll** method in the **Collection<E>** interface is an example. Its parameter type is **Collection<? extends E>**, which means that the parameter can be a collection of any class that inherits from class **E**.

If you need to perform some action for each item in the collection, you can use a simplified **for** loop. The following example shows how to print each string in a vector of **String** objects:

```
Vector<String> v = new Vector<String>();
for (String s : v) {
        System.out.println(s);
}
```

This type of **for** loop can be used with any of the collection classes and can also be used with arrays.

ArrayList<E> Class

The **ArrayList** class implements the **List** interface. It also implements the **RandomAccess** interface, which means that elements anywhere in the list can be accessed quickly. List elements are stored in an underlying array, which grows as necessary to accommodate additional elements.

Although **ArrayList** and **LinkedList** both implement the **List** interface, there are important differences in how they are used. An **ArrayList** works well where any element in the list can be accessed at any time, and where the size of the list does not change often.

A **LinkedList**, on the other hand, does not provide efficient access to elements that are not the first (or last) on the list. However, it works well in situations where elements are frequently added to the beginning (or end) of the list.

An **ArrayList** object has a method for accessing the size (number of elements) of the list, as do other lists and collections, but it also has a method for setting the capacity of the list. The capacity tells how many elements can fit in the underlying array without allocating additional space. By using the appropriate constructor and the **ensureCapacity** method, you can avoid numerous small increases in the capacity of the array. Bear in mind that the capacity of the **ArrayList** is important only for performance reasons, and you can ignore it if the performance of your program is acceptable.

Constructors

- **ArrayList()**

This constructor creates an empty list with initial capacity of ten.

- **ArrayList(Collection<? extends E> coll)**

This constructor makes a list and adds the elements of **coll** to the new list. The capacity of the list will be the size of **coll** plus an additional 10 percent.

- **ArrayList(int initialCapacity)**

This constructor makes an empty list with the initial capacity of **initialCapacity**.

Methods   Only methods that differ from those in the **List** and **Collection** interfaces are described here.

- **void ensureCapacity(int capacity)**

This method makes the capacity of the list at least as big as its parameter.

- **void trimToSize()**

This method reduces the capacity of the list to the list's current size.

Arrays Class

The **Arrays** class provides implementations for various algorithms used with arrays. All the methods in this class are static. Some of the methods in **Arrays** are generic methods. See the description of the **Collections** class (also in **java.util**) for a short explanation of generic methods. The **Collections** description also briefly explains the **Comparable** and **Comparator** interfaces, which are used with sorting and searching methods in the **Arrays** class.

Most of the methods in this class take an array as a parameter (**equals** takes two arrays of the same type) and are overloaded so that there is a version of the method for each primitive type. There is one **sort** method that sorts an array of **byte** values, another that sorts an array of **char** values, and so on for the other primitive types: **double**, **float**, **int**, **long**, and **short**. A few methods (**equals**, **fill**, and **toString**) take a parameter that is an array of **boolean** values, but **sort** and **binarySearch** do not.

Methods

- **static int binarySearch(byte[] a, byte key)**
- **static int binarySearch(char[] a, char key)**
- **static int binarySearch(double[] a, double key)**
- **static int binarySearch(float[] a, float key)**
- **static int binarySearch(int[] a, int key)**
- **static int binarySearch(long[] a, long key)**

- `static int binarySearch(short[] a, short key)`
- `static int binarySearch(Object[] a, Object key)`

Binary search is an efficient way to find out where a particular item (called the *key*) is in a sorted list of items. Each of these methods returns an **int** value that gives the index of the key (the second parameter) in the array (the first parameter). If the key is not in the array the method returns a negative value. The array must be sorted to get correct results.

- `static <T>`
  `int binarySearch(T[] a, T key, Comparator<? super T> c)`

This version of **binarySearch** is a generic method. See the description of the **Collections** class (in **java.util**) for a short explanation of generic methods and of the **Comparator** interface.

- `static boolean equals(boolean[] a1, boolean[] a2)`
- `static boolean equals(byte[] a1, byte[] a2)`
- `static boolean equals(char[] a1, char[] a2)`
- `static boolean equals(double[] a1, double [] a2)`
- `static boolean equals(float[] a1, float[] a2)`
- `static boolean equals(int[] a1, int[] a2)`
- `static boolean equals(long[] a1, long[] a2)`
- `static boolean equals(short[] a1, short[] a2)`
- `static boolean equals(Object[] a1, Object[] a2)`

The **equals** method returns **true** if its two parameters have the same number of elements and corresponding elements have the same value. It will return **true** if passed two **null** array references.

- `static void fill(byte[] a, byte fillVal)`
- `static void fill(char[] a, char fillVal)`
- `static void fill(double[] a, double fillVal)`
- `static void fill(float[] a, float fillVal)`
- `static void fill(int[] a, int fillVal)`
- `static void fill(long[] a, long fillVal)`
- `static void fill(short[] a, short fillVal)`
- `static void fill(Object[] a, Object fillVal)`

This method puts the same value in all the elements of an array. The array to fill is the first parameter, and the fill value is the second parameter.

In addition to the **fill** methods listed here, there are additional overloaded methods that allow a range of an array to be filled. These methods take second and third **int** parameters that specify the beginning and ending indices for the range to be filled. The fill value is the last (fourth) parameter for these methods.

- `static void sort(byte[] a)`
- `static void sort(char[] a)`
- `static void sort(double[] a)`
- `static void sort(float[] a)`

- `static void sort(int[] a)`
- `static void sort(long[] a)`
- `static void sort(short[] a)`

The **sort** method puts the array elements in ascending numerical order (smaller elements first). In the case of char values, the first lower-case letter comes after the last upper-case letter, so '**a**' comes after '**Z**'.

- `static void sort(Object[] a)`

This method sorts an array of objects. Each object in the array must implement the interface **Comparable**.

- `static <T> void sort(T[] a, Comparator<? super T> c)`

This version of **sort** is a generic method. See the description of the **Collections** class (in **java.util**) for a short explanation of generic methods and of the **Comparator** interface.

In addition to the **sort** methods listed here, there are additional overloaded methods that allow a range of an array to be sorted. These methods take second and third **int** parameters that specify the beginning and ending indices for the range to be sorted.

Example   This code demonstrates using the **sort** method with an array of characters. Because the numerical value of a lower-case letter is greater than the numerical value of any upper-case letter, '**a**' comes after '**Z**' even though it comes first alphabetically.

This code uses the simplified **for** loop that was added to Java in version 1.5.

```
char[] a = new char[3];

a[0] = 'a';
a[1] = 'Z';
a[2] = 'A';

Arrays.sort(a);
for (char c : a) {
    System.out.print(c + " ");
}
System.out.println();
```

The output from executing this code is:
```
A Z a
```

Collection<E> Interface

The **Collection** interface is the most general representation of a group of objects in Java. Its implementing classes include **ArrayList**, **LinkedList**, **HashSet**, **Stack**, **TreeSet**, and **Vector**. Objects in the collection will be instances of the class specified by the **E** type parameter.

Methods that change the collection are considered optional. In other words, not every class that implements the **Collection** interface will allow modifications. If a modification method is called from a class that does not allow modification, an **UnsupportedOperationException** will occur.

Methods

- `boolean add(E item)`

This method adds `item` to the collection. Since this method modifies the collection, it is optional and not every implementing class will implement it.

- `boolean addAll(Collection<? extends E> coll)`

This method will add all of the objects in the parameter to the calling object. It is an optional operation.

- `void clear()`

This method removes all the items from the collection. It is an optional operation.

- `boolean contains(Object item)`

This method returns `true` if `item` is in the calling object.

- `boolean containsAll(Collection<?> coll)`

This method returns `true` if all the items in the parameter are contained in the calling object.

- `boolean equals(Object obj)`

The meaning of this method depends on the implementation. In some cases it will return `true` only if `obj` and the calling object are references to the same instances. In other cases it will compare values. Consult the documentation for the implementation to find out how this method works for that class.

- `boolean isEmpty()`

This method returns `true` if the calling object has no elements in it.

- `Iterator<E> iterator()`

This method returns an iterator over the elements in the calling object.

- `boolean remove(Object o)`

This method removes `obj` from the collection if it is present. It is an optional operation.

- `boolean removeAll(Collection<?> coll)`

This method removes all the objects in `coll` from the calling object. It is an optional operation.

- `boolean retainAll(Collection<?> coll)`

This method removes all the objects in the calling object that are not in `coll`. It is an optional operation.

- `int size()`

This method returns the number of elements in the calling object.

- `Object[] toArray()`

This method returns an array that includes all the objects in the calling object. The elements in the array will be in the same order in which they would be returned by an iterator.

- `<T>[] toArray(T[] a)`

This method returns an array that includes all the objects in the calling object. The elements in the returned array will be the same type as the elements in the parameter. The elements in the array will be in the same order that they would be returned by an iterator.

Collections Class

The `Collections` class provides implementations for a number of useful algorithms related to collections. All the methods in this class are static.

Most of the methods in this class are generic methods. A generic method has a type parameter in the declaration. For instance, one of the `max` methods in the `Collections` class is declared like this:

```
public static <T> T max(Collection<? extends T> coll,
                        Comparator<? super T> comp)
```

The `<T>` following `static` is a type parameter. When the method is called, the compiler determines the value of the type parameter, `T`, by examining the types of the parameters to the methods. If `coll` is a collection of strings, and `comp` is a comparator for strings, then the value of the type parameter will be `String` and the return value of `max` will be a `String` object.

Many of the methods in this class make use of two interfaces called `Comparable` and `Comparator`. For example, there are two versions of the sort method, one where the class of the elements implements `Comparable`, and one where an object called a comparator (which implements the `Comparator` interface) is passed in as a parameter.

When a class implements the `Comparable` interface, it defines a natural ordering. For example, numeric classes (like `Integer`) have a natural ordering where smaller numbers precede larger ones. The `String` and `Date` classes are two other classes that have natural orderings and implement the `Comparable` interface. When a natural ordering exists and you want to use it, you can use the version of the `sort` method that does not take a comparator as a parameter. The type parameter (at the beginning of the method heading) specifies that the element type must be comparable.

The `WordCount` program in the **Complete Examples** section uses a class that implements the `Comparable` interface and another class that implements the `Comparator` interface.

If you don't want to use the natural ordering, or if there isn't one for the element type, then you will need to pass in an additional parameter that tells how to compare two elements. For instance, if you want to sort a list of integers in descending order rather than ascending order, you need to pass in a comparator instead of using the natural ordering.

Methods

- `static <T extends Object & Comparable<? super T>>`
  `int binarySearch(List<? extends T> list, T key)`
- `static <T> int binarySearch(List<? extends T> list,`
  `T key, Comparator<? super T> c)`

Binary search is an efficient way to find out where a particular item (called the *key*) is in a sorted list of items. Each of these methods returns an `int` value that gives the index of the key (the second parameter) in the list (the first parameter). If the key is not in the list the method returns a negative value. The list must be sorted to get correct results.

The first **binarySearch** method can be used when the elements of the list are instances of a class that implements the **Comparable** interface. The second method is used when the elements are not **Comparable** or when a different comparison (for example, descending rather than ascending) is needed.

- ```
  static <T> void copy(List<? super T> dest,
                       List<? extends T> src)
  ```

This method copies the second parameter (the source list) to the first parameter (the destination list). The destination list must be at least as long as the source list.

- ```
  static <T extends Object & Comparable<? super T>>
         T max(Collection<? extends T> coll)
  ```

- ```
  static <T>
         T max(Collection<? extends T> coll,
               Comparator<? super T> comp)
  ```

- ```
  static <T extends Object & Comparable<? super T>>
         T min(Collection<? extends T> coll)
  ```

- ```
  static <T>
         T min(Collection<? extends T> coll,
               Comparator<? super T> comp)
  ```

These methods return the maximum and minimum values from a collection. The return type of the method will be the type of the collection elements. The two-parameter versions are used if there is no natural ordering (the element class doesn't implement **Comparable**) or if a different ordering than the natural one is needed.

- ```
  static void shuffle(List<?> list)
  ```

- ```
  static void shuffle(List<?> list, Random rnd)
  ```

The shuffle method randomly reorders the elements in a list.

- ```
  static <T extends Comparable<? super T>>
         void sort(List<T> list)
  ```

- ```
  static <T>
         void sort(List<T> list, Comparator<? super T> c)
  ```

The preceding sorting methods can be used with implementations of the **List** interface. The first method requires the type of the list elements to be **Comparable**, and the second requires an object that implements the **Comparator** interface to be passed in as a parameter. A list of strings, numbers, or dates can be sorted by the one-parameter version, because the classes for these kinds of value implement the **Comparable** interface.

Note that the one-parameter version of sort will sort in ascending order, so if you want elements sorted in descending order, you will need to make a comparator and pass it to the two-parameter version of sort.

The **WordCount** application in the **Complete Examples** section uses both of the **sort** methods listed here.
  ```

Enumeration<E> Interface

The **Enumeration** interface provides a way to systematically access a group of elements. The **Iterator** interface is similar to this one, but has shorter method names and so might be preferable.

Methods

- **boolean hasMoreElements()**

  This method returns **true** if there are elements in the group that have not yet been accessed.

- **E nextElement()**

  This method returns the next element from the group. If all the elements in the group have already been returned, this method will throw the **NoSuchElement-Exception**.

HashMap<K,V> Class

This class uses a hash table to implement the **Map** interface.

  The **WordCount** application in the **Complete Examples** section uses the **HashMap** class.

Constructors

- **HashMap()**
- **HashMap(Map<? extends K, ? extends V> coll)**
- **HashMap(int initCapacity, float loadFactor)**
- **HashMap(int initCapacity)**

  Constructors that don't specify a load factor use the default of 0.75. See the description of the **Hashtable** class for more information on load factors. If the initial capacity is not set by a parameter, it will be the default of 16.

Methods   See the description of the **Map** interface for information about the methods of this class.

HashSet<E> Class

This class uses a hash table to implement the **Set** interface. The elements in the set are not in any particular order, and the order of iteration may change from one time to the next. This implementation allows null elements in the set.

Constructors

- **HashSet()**
- **HashSet(Collection<? extends E> coll)**
- **HashSet(int initCapacity, float loadFactor)**
- **HashSet(int initCapacity)**

  Constructors that don't specify a load factor use the default of 0.75. See the description of the **Hashtable** class for more information on load factors. If the initial capacity is not set by a parameter, it will be the default of 16.

Methods   See the descriptions for the **Set** and **Collection** interfaces for information about the methods of this class.

Hashtable<K, V> Class

Hash tables are useful for storing and retrieving values that are associated with keys. For example, directory information for students, such as name, address, and phone number, could be a value stored under the key of the student's ID number.

The class **Hashtable** implements the **Map** interface.

The **Hashtable** has two type parameters, one for the type of the keys, and one for the type of the values.

Constructors   Two important issues in making a new hash table are the initial capacity and the load. The initial capacity tells how many buckets there are in the table when it is created. In general, a larger number of buckets means faster access but requires more space.

The load factor tells what fraction of the capacity must be in use before the table is expanded. The default value for the load factor is 0.75, which means that when 75 percent of the capacity is in use, the table will be expanded. Setting a lower load factor will give faster access to the values in the table but requires more space.

- **Hashtable()**
This constructor creates a hash table with the default initial capacity and the default load factor.

- **Hashtable(int initialCapacity)**
This constructor creates a hash table with the specified initial capacity and the default load factor.

- **Hashtable(int initialCapacity, float loadFactor)**
This constructor creates a hash table with the specified initial capacity and load factor.

- **Hashtable(Map mapping)**
This constructor creates a hash table with the same entries as **mapping**. The initial capacity of the new table will be twice the capacity required for **mapping**.

Methods

- **boolean contains(Object value)**
This method returns **true** if the table contains **value**.

- **boolean containsKey(Object key)**
This method returns **true** if the table contains the key specified as the parameter.

- **Enumeration elements()**
This method returns an enumeration of the values stored in the table. This method is useful for things like printing out a list of all the values in the table. **Enumeration** is an interface defined in the **java.util** package.

- **Enumeration<V> elements()**
When a **Hashtable** object is created using a type parameter, **v**, for the values, then the enumeration returned by the elements method will be that type.

- **`Object get(Object key)`**

This method is used to look up the value associated with **key** in the table. In most cases you will want to use a cast to convert the reference returned by this method. For example, if you are using the table to store strings, then you would use a cast to convert the reference to a String reference, like this:

```
String address = (String) myTable.get("Jane Doe");
```

- **`V get(Object key)`**

When a **`Hashtable`** object is created using a type parameter, **v**, for the values, then the value returned by get will be of type **v**, and no type casting is required to assign it to a variable of type **v**. For example, if **v** is **`String`**, then a statement like the following one can copy the reference stored in the **`Hashtable`** to a **`String`** variable:

```
String address = myTable.get("Jane Doe");
```
In this example **k** also happens to be **`String`**.

- **`Object put(Object key, Object value)`**

This method associates **value** with **key** in the hash table.

- **`V put(K key, V value)`**

When used with type parameters, **put** takes a parameter of type **k** (the class for keys in the **`Hashtable`**) and a parameter of type **v** (the class for values) and returns a value of type **v**.

- **`Object remove(Object key)`**

This method removes **key** and its corresponding value from the hash table. The value returned by this method is the value associated with **key**. If **key** is not associated with any value, the method returns **`null`**.

LinkedList<E> Class

This class implements the **`List`**, **`Queue`**, and **`Collection`** interfaces. The underlying representation is a list where each element in the list has a pointer (or link) to the next element. The linked structure works well for adding elements to the beginning (and end) of the list, but is less efficient for nonsequential access. If it is important to efficiently access the elements of the list in any order, consider using **`ArrayList`** rather than **`LinkedList`**.

Constructors

- **`LinkedList()`**
- **`LinkedList(Collection<? extends E> coll)`**

This constructor makes a list that includes all the elements of **coll**.

Methods   This section only describes methods that differ from the **`List`** and **`Collection`** interfaces.

- **`void addFirst(E item)`**
- **`void addLast(E item)`**

These two methods add **item** to the beginning and end of the list, respectively.

- **E getFirst()**
- **E getLast()**

These methods return the first and last elements of the list.

- **E removeFirst()**
- **E removeLast()**

These methods remove and return the first and last elements of the list.

List<E> Interface

A list is an ordered collection where elements can be accessed by their position in the list. Duplicate items are usually allowed in a list. Some classes that implement the **List** interface are **ArrayList**, **LinkedList**, and **Vector**. Elements in the list will be instances of the class specified by the type parameter **E**.

The **Collections** class contains several useful methods for lists, including **binarySearch**, **sort**, and **shuffle**.

The **WordCount** program in the **Complete Examples** section shows an example of using the **List** interface.

Methods   See the description of the **Collection** interface for additional methods. The methods listed here are either not part of the **Collection** interface (such as **indexOf**) or are changed from the ones in the **Collection** interface (such as **add**, which specifies the position of added elements).

Methods that have an index parameter can throw the **IndexOutOfBoundsException** if the index is out of range.

- **boolean add(E item)**
- **void add(int index, E item)**

For the first version of the **add** method, the new element is added at the end of the list. The position of the new element in the list is specified for the second **add** method.

- **E remove(int index)**

This method removes the element at the specified index. Elements that follow the removed element will be shifted one place to the left.

- **int indexOf(Object o)**
- **int lastIndexOf(Object o)**

These methods return the index of an item in the list. If there is more than one occurrence, **indexOf** returns the index of the first occurrence (smallest index) and **lastIndexOf** returns the index of the last occurrence (largest index).

- **List<E> subList(int fromIndex, int toIndex)**

This method returns a list of the elements in the calling object, beginning at **fromIndex** and going up to (but not including) **toIndex**. Nonstructural changes to the returned list will be reflected in the original list, and vice versa. Structural changes to the original list can cause unpredictable results.

Iterator<E> Interface

Like the **Enumeration** interface, this interface provides methods to systematically access the members of a group of objects.

Methods

- **boolean hasNext()**

This method returns **true** if there are elements in the group that have not yet been accessed.

- **E next()**

This method returns the next element from the group. If all of the elements in the group have already been returned, this method will throw the **NoSuchElement-Exception**.

- **void remove()**

This method removes the most recently accessed element of the group. This is an optional operation, so some classes that implement the **Iterator** interface might not implement this method. If this method has not been implemented but is called, an **UnsupportedOperationException** will occur.

Map<K,V> Interface

Maps are used to associate keys with values. When you add a value to the map, you specify a key for it. Later you can use the same key to retrieve the value. The **K** type parameter is the type of the keys, and the **V** type parameter is the type of the values.

Some implementations of **Map** do not allow destructive operations, and some don't allow null keys or values.

Hashtable is one class that implements the **Map** interface.

The **WordCount** program in the **Complete Examples** section shows an example of using the **Map** interface. In that program, the key type (**K**) is **String**, and the value type (**V**) is **Integer**.

Methods

- **boolean containsKey(Object key)**

This method returns **true** if the parameter is a key (has a value associated with it) in the calling object.

- **boolean containsValue(Object value)**

This method returns **true** if the parameter is a value (is associated with a key) in the calling object.

- **V get(Object key)**

The **get** method returns the value associated with the parameter. If there is no value associated with the parameter, the return value will be **null**.

- **Set<K> keySet()**

This method returns all of the keys in the **Map** as elements of a set.

- **V put(K key, V value)**

This method associates **value** with **key** in the **Map**. If **key** is associated with a different value before the method is called, that association will be lost.

- **V remove(Object key)**

This method removes its parameter and its associated value from the **Map**. The return value will be the value formerly associated with **key**.

- **Collection<V> values()**

This method returns all of the values in the **Map** as a **Collection**.

Set<E> Interface

A set is a collection where duplicate elements are not allowed. The elements in a mathematical set are not ordered, but some Java set implementations have ordered elements. Two classes that implement the **Set** interface are **HashSet** and **TreeSet**. Elements in the set will be instances of the class specified by the type parameter, **E**.

Methods See the description of the **Collection** interface for additional methods.

- **boolean add(E item)**
- **boolean addAll(Collection<? extends E> coll)**

These methods are the same as the **add** methods for **Collection** except that they do not add elements that are already in the set.

Stack<E> Class

The **Stack** class inherits from the **Vector** class, but also has methods for the typical operations of the stack abstract data type. In a stack, the last item put into the stack is the first one to come out, so they are sometimes called LIFO (last-in-first-out) data types.

Constructor

- **Stack()**

This constructor makes an empty stack.

Methods

- **boolean empty()**

This method returns **true** if the stack is empty.

- **E peek()**

This method returns the object at the top of the stack, but does not remove it from the stack.

- **E pop()**

This method returns the object at the top of the stack and removes it from the stack.

- **E push(E item)**

This method adds **item** to the top of the stack. The return value is **item**.

Example The stack in this example is created with a type parameter of **Object**, so it can have instances of any class pushed onto it. Because of the autoboxing feature added to Java version 1.5, the **Integer** constructor does not have to be used when the numbers 1 through 4 are pushed onto the stack. Likewise, because of the auto-unboxing feature added to Java 1.5, the **intValue** method of **Integer** does not have to be explicitly called. However, the value popped off the stack must be cast as an **Integer** or auto-unboxing will not occur.

In the output, note that the first word popped onto the stack, "apple," is the last word popped off the stack and therefore the last word printed. Likewise, 1 is the first number pushed onto the stack and the last number printed before the total, 10.

```
Stack<Object> myStack = new Stack<Object>();
int total = 0, item;

myStack.push("apple");
myStack.push("bird");
myStack.push("cat");
while (!myStack.empty()) {
     System.out.println(myStack.pop());
}

myStack.push(1);
myStack.push(2);
myStack.push(3);
myStack.push(4);
while (!myStack.empty()) {
     item = (Integer)myStack.pop();
     System.out.println(item);
     total += item;
}
System.out.println(total);
```

Output
```
cat
bird
apple
4
3
2
1
10
```

Vector<E> Class

A vector is similar to an array in that it contains a number of components that can be accessed by an index number. The capacity of a vector, however, can change dynamically, whereas the capacity of an array is fixed when it is created.

The components, or elements, of a vector are references to **Objects**. Therefore, when an object is retrieved, its reference is usually cast to the type of object stored in the vector. Since all classes extend **Object**, the components of a vector can be instances of different classes. However, using a vector will be simpler and easier if all of the components are the same class, have a common base class (other than **Object**), or implement one interface.

The **Vector** class implements the **Collection** and **List** interfaces.

As of version 1.5 of Java, the **Vector** class can be used with generic types. When a vector is created with a type parameter **E**, the compiler uses **E** as the type of the vector's elements. Many of the methods (such as **add**) take parameters of the element type **E**, and methods like **get** return objects of type **E** rather than type **Object**.

Constructors

- `Vector()`
- `Vector(int initialCapacity)`
- `Vector(int initialCapacity, int capacityIncrement)`

The first two constructors have a default capacity increment that doubles the capacity of the vector or whenever it gets full. A vector created by the first constructor will have the default capacity of 10 objects.

- `Vector(Collection c)`

This method copies references of all elements in **c** to the new vector. Note that **Vector** implements **Collection**, so this constructor can be used to make a copy of a vector.

Methods

- `boolean add(E obj)`

This method appends the parameter to the end of the vector. **E** is the type parameter specified when the vector was created.

- `Enumeration elements()`

This method returns an enumeration of the components of the vector.

- `Enumeration<E> elements()`

When the vector is created with a type parameter **E**, the **elements** method returns an enumeration parameterized by the element type **E**.

- `E get(int index)`

This method retrieves the component that is stored at the specified **index** in the vector.

- `E set(int index, E element`

This method makes **element** the new component at **index**. The replaced component is the returned value of the method.

- `<T> T[] toArray(T[] a)`

This method returns an array containing the components from the vector. Elements in the array will be in the same order as in the vector.

The parameter **a** can be an array of any class, and the returned value will be an array of the same type. For example, if the vector contains strings, **a** could be an array of type **String[]**, and the strings in the result could be used as **String** objects without casting.

- `boolean contains(Object elem)`

This method returns **true** if the vector contains the component referenced by **elem**.

- `int indexOf(Object elem)`
- `int indexOf(Object elem, int index)`

This method returns the index of **elem** if that element is in the vector. If the element is not in the vector, the return value will be –1. The second **indexOf** method begins searching at **index** rather than at the beginning of the vector.

- `void clear()`

This method removes all of the elements from the vector.

- **E remove(int index)**

This method removes the element stored at the specified index from the vector.

- **boolean isEmpty()**

This method returns true if there are no components in the vector.

- **int size()**

This method returns the number of components in the vector.

Example   In the following code, a vector is created with **Integer** as the type parameter, so the elements of the vector will be **Integer**. Even though the **add** method takes **Integer** parameters, because of the autoboxing feature (added to Java in version 1.5), the integer literals will be automatically converted to **Integer** objects.

This example uses two methods from the **Collections** class: **max** and **sort**. It also uses the simplified **for** loop (added to Java in version 1.5) to print out the vector elements.

```
Vector<Integer> v = new Vector<Integer>();
v.add(42);
v.add(38);
v.add(99);

System.out.println("The max is: " + Collections.max(v));

System.out.println("Unsorted values:");
for (Integer i : v) {
    System.out.println(i);
}

Collections.sort(v);
System.out.println("Sorted values:");
for (Integer i : v) {
    System.out.println(i);
}
```

Output

```
The max is: 99
Unsorted values:
42
38
99
Sorted values:
38
42
99
```

javax.swing Package

The Swing package provides lightweight versions of many of the original AWT components. Lightweight components allow an interface to be consistent across platforms, since they do not rely on any platform's implementations of the components. Many of the Swing component classes start with **J** to distinguish them from the corresponding components in the AWT. For example, the lightweight button class is called `JButton` instead of `Button`.

In many ways, using Swing components is similar to using AWT components, except that Swing components generally have more capabilities. For instance, Swing labels can include pictures (icons), whereas AWT labels cannot. Another important difference is that `JFrame` and `JApplet` containers have a content pane. Most components are added to the content pane instead of to the frame or the applet itself. The `SpotlightApplet` example in the **Complete Examples** section shows how a component can be added to a content frame.

To learn more about using Swing components, you can read the Java Tutorial about user interfaces. It is available at http://java.sun.com/docs/books/tutorial/uiswing/index.html.

BoxLayout Class

The **BoxLayout** manager can be thought of as a grid with only one row or one column. However, a grid layout has a set number of rows and columns, whereas a box can take any number of components.

Constants

- `static int X_AXIS`
This constant is used to specify a horizontal arrangement.

- `static int Y_AXIS`
This constant is used to specify a vertical arrangement.

Constructor

- `BoxLayout(Container target, int axis)`
The second parameter is one of the constants `X_AXIS` (horizontal arrangement) or `Y_AXIS` (vertical arrangement).

ButtonGroup Class

This class can be used to group radio buttons (`JRadioButton`). Only one button in the group can be selected at a time. If a button is selected and the user clicks on a different button, then the first button will be deselected.

Constructors

- `ButtonGroup()`

Methods

- `void add(AbstractButton b)`
- `int getButtonCount()`
- `Enumeration getElements()`
- `void remove(AbstractButton b)`

ImageIcon Class

An icon is a fixed-size picture that can be added to many kinds of Swing components. The **ImageIcon** class implements the **Icon** interface, and so provides a way to add pictures to components like labels and buttons.

Constructors   The **description** parameter to these constructors is for a text description of the image.

- **ImageIcon(Image image)**
- **ImageIcon(Image image, String description)**

This constructor creates an icon from an **Image** object.

- **ImageIcon(String path)**
- **ImageIcon(String path, String description)**

This constructor creates an icon from a file. The **path** parameter can be just a file name, or it can be a path including one or more directories.

- **ImageIcon(URL location)**
- **ImageIcon(URL location, String description)**

This constructor creates an icon from a URL (Web resource).

Methods

- **int getIconHeight()**
- **int getIconWidth()**

These two methods get the height and width of the image in pixels.

- **String getDescription()**
- **void setDescription(String description)**
- **Image getImage()**
- **void setImage(Image image)**

Example

```
ImageIcon icon = new ImageIcon("lighthouse.jpg");
JLabel label = new JLabel("Lighthouse", icon, JLabel.CENTER);
```

In this example the path is just a file name, but it could include directories also, like **"images/lighthouse.jpg"**.

JApplet Class

The **JApplet** class extends the **Applet** class, so methods like **getImage** and **getDocumentBase** are available in **JApplet** also. However, there are some important differences. One difference is that you use JFC/Swing components rather than AWT components. Another difference is that a **JApplet** uses a content pane, whereas an **Applet** does not. Components in a **JApplet** should be added to the content pane rather than to the applet itself. Setting the layout and removing components are also done to the content pane. Note that the default layout manager for a **JApplet** is the border layout, unlike the default layout for an **Applet**, which is a flow layout.

An applet that is not a **JApplet** can contain a **paint** method used to draw shapes and images, but **JApplet**s should use other techniques. One alternative to using the **paint** method to draw images is to use a component that can include an icon, like **JLabel**. Another alternative is to add another component to the applet's content pane and have it implement **paintComponent**. The **SpotlightApplet** example in the **Complete Examples** section shows a small program that uses the latter approach. In addition to using a **JPanel** to draw an image, the **SpotlightApplet** also shows an example of adding a component to the content pane.

Methods

- **Container getContentPane()**
This method returns the content pane for the applet. Components are added to the content pane rather than the applet itself. The layout is set for the content pane also. For example, to set the layout to be flow layout, you could use code like this:

```
getContentPane().setLayout(new FlowLayout());
```

JButton Class

This class inherits from **AbstractButton**, **JComponent**, **Container**, and **Component**. Methods inherited from these classes allow you to retrieve or set various properties, including the text, font, icon, and foreground and background colors.

Your program can tell when a button has been pushed if you add an **ActionListener** to the button. Use **addActionListener**, an inherited method, to add the listener.

The **SpotlightApplet** example (in the **Complete Examples** section) includes a **JButton** object.

Constructors

- **JButton()**
- **JButton(Icon icon)**
- **JButton(String text)**
- **JButton(String text, Icon icon)**
Constructors can take an icon, a string, or both, as parameters. The icon and text can be retrieved or set later using inherited methods.

JCheckBox Class

A check box is a GUI component that the user can select or deselect. Check boxes are often used to allow a user to turn options on and off. If only one option from a group may be selected, use the **JRadioButton** and **ButtonGroup** classes rather than **JCheckBox**.

This class inherits from **JToggleButton**, which in turn inherits from the **AbstractButton** class.

Constructors

- **JCheckBox()**
- **JCheckBox(Icon icon)**

- `JCheckBox(Icon icon, boolean selected)`
- `JCheckBox(String text)`
- `JCheckBox(String text, boolean selected)`
- `JCheckBox(String text, Icon icon)`
- `JCheckBox(String text, Icon icon, boolean selected)`

The constructors allow the text, icon, and state (`selected`) to be specified. The default state is `false` (not selected).

Methods

- `boolean isSelected()`
- `void setSelected(boolean b)`

These two methods are inherited from the `AbstractButton` class and may be used to retrieve or set the state of the check box.

As an instance of a descendant class of `AbstractButton`, a check box can be associated with several kinds of listeners. Listeners are added using the following inherited methods:

- `void addActionListener(ActionListener 1)`
- `void addChangeListener(ChangeListener 1)`
- `void addItemListener(ItemListener 1)`

JComboBox Class

An uneditable combo box is similar to a menu, but is activated by a small button next to a display of the current selection. When the user clicks the small button, a drop-down list appears that shows a number of items the user can select. Only one item may be selected at a time.

An editable combo box is a combination of a text field and a drop-down list. The user can type in a value or select a value from the drop-down list. You can set the combo box to be editable or not by using the `setEditable` method listed below.

This class implements the following interfaces (among others): `ActionListener`, `EventListener`, `ItemSelectable`, and `MenuContainer`.

Constructors

- `JComboBox()`
- `JComboBox(ComboBoxModel combo)`
- `JComboBox(Object[] items)`
- `JComboBox(Vector items)`

The main question for `JComboBox` constructors is: Where do the items for the new combo box come from? The first constructor, which has no parameters, creates a combo box with no items. The second gets the items from an existing combo box. (Note that `JComboBox` implements `ComboBoxModel`.) The third gets the items from an array, and the fourth from a vector.

Methods

- **`void addItem(Object anObject)`**
This method adds **item** to the end of the drop-down list.

- **`Object getItemAt(int index)`**
This method returns the item at the given **index**. If the index is not valid (less than zero or greater than the number of items in the list), the returned value will be **null**.

- **`int getItemCount()`**
This method returns the number of items in the drop-down list.

- **`Object getSelectedItem()`**
This method returns the item that the user selected from the drop-down list.

- **`void insertItemAt(Object item, int index)`**
This method adds **item** to the drop-down list at the place specified by **index**.

- **`boolean isEditable()`**
This method indicates whether or not the combo box is editable. If it is editable, the selection is displayed in a text field, which the user can change directly by typing in a new value. If it is not editable, the user can only change the value by choosing a different selection from the drop-down list.

- **`void removeAllItems()`**
This method removes all the items from the drop-down list.

- **`void removeItem(Object item)`**
This method removes the object that is equal to the item from the drop-down list.

- **`void removeItemAt(int index)`**
This method removes the item at **index** from the drop-down list.

- **`void setEditable(boolean editable)`**
This method sets the combo box to be editable (meaning that the user can type in a new value) or not (the user can only select from the drop-down list).

- **`void setSelectedIndex(int index)`**
This method marks the item at **index** as the selected item, as if the user had chosen it from the drop-down list.

- **`void setSelectedItem(Object item)`**
This method marks the item equal to **item** as the selected item, as if the user had chosen it from the drop-down list.
Each of the following methods allows a listener to be added to the combo box:

- **`void addActionListener(ActionListener 1)`**
- **`void addItemListener(ItemListener aListener)`**

JComponent Class

This is the parent class for many of the Swing components. It inherits from **Container** in the AWT package, which in turn inherits from the AWT **Component** class.

JComponent has a large number of methods, but this description will focus on a few that are not available in AWT components.

Methods

- **void paintComponent(Graphics g)**

You can override this method if you want your program to paint a component directly. Note that in Swing you would not override the **paint** method as you do with AWT components such as **Canvas**. If you override this method, you should not make permanent changes to the Graphics object that is passed in as a parameter. Instead you can make a copy to change.

If the component is opaque, you must be sure to paint all the pixels within it boundaries. You can determine the boundaries of the component by using the **getWidth** and **getHeight** methods.

- **int getWidth()**
- **int getHeight()**

These methods return the width or height of the component in pixels.

- **String getToolTipText()**
- **void setToolTipText(String text)**

A tool tip is text that appears above a component when the user holds the cursor above the component. The text gives the user information about how to use the component. Tool tips can easily be added to Swing components by passing in the text as a parameter to the **setToolTipText** method.

- **boolean getOpaque()**
- **void setOpaque(boolean isOpaque)**

If a **JComponent** is declared as opaque, then components behind it will not be painted. If you make a class that inherits from **JComponent**, and declare it as opaque, you must be sure to paint all of the pixels within the component's boundaries. Keep in mind that making a component nonopaque means that the program will spend more time painting, because all the components behind a nonopaque component must be painted, whereas components behind an opaque component do not have to be painted.

- **Border getBorder()**
- **void setBorder(Border border)**

These methods are used to get and set the borders of the component. The class **javax.swing.BorderFactory** provides static methods that can be used to make borders.

JDialog Class

This class can be used to create and display a dialog window. Dialog windows are top-level containers, which means that most components should be added to the content pane of the window rather than to the window directly.

An alternative to using the **JDialog** class is to use the **JOptionPane** class instead. The **JOptionPane** class provides static methods for displaying standard types of dialog windows, such as message windows and confirmation windows.

This class inherits from **java.awt.Dialog**.

Constructors

- **JDialog(Frame owner)**
- **JDialog(Frame owner, boolean modal)**
- **JDialog(Frame owner, String title)**
- **JDialog(Frame owner, String title, boolean modal)**

There are additional constructors that correspond to these but have **Dialog** as the class of the owner rather than **Frame**. Constructors that do not have the **modal** parameter will not be modal. A modal dialog does not allow the user to do anything with any other window in the program until it has been closed.

Methods

- **Container getContentPane()**
- **void setContentPane(Container contentPane)**

The inherited methods **setSize** and **show** are used to make the dialog visible on the screen. The following methods (among others) are inherited from **Dialog** and its ancestor classes, **Window**, **Container**, and **Component**:

- **void setSize(Dimension d)**
- **void setSize(int width, int height)**

Example   The following code shows a dialog box that is created using a constructor with only one parameter, which is the parent frame. A label is added to the content pane of the dialog, and then inherited methods are used to set the size and display the window.

```
dialog = new JDialog(this);
dlabel = new JLabel("This is a dialog window.");
dialog.getContentPane().add(dlabel);
dialog.setSize(200, 50);
dialog.show();
```

JFileChooser Class

The **JFileChooser** class provides a consistent way for a program to allow users to select a program. Users can browse the computer's file system to find the file that they are looking for.

Constants

- **static int CANCEL_OPTION**
- **static int APPROVE_OPTION**

These two constants are two possible return values from the show methods listed below.

Constructors

- **JFileChooser()**
- **JFileChooser(File currentDirectory)**

- **JFileChooser(String currentDirectoryPath)**

The first of these constructors opens a file dialog box in a default directory. If you want the chooser to open from a particular directory, you can specify the directory with either a **File** object or a **String**.

- **void setFileFilter(FileFilter filter)**

Sets the file filter, which determines what types of files will be shown in the selection window. The parameter to this method is a **FileFilter**. There is no default **FileFilter** implementation, so if you want to use a file filter you must write a class that inherits from the abstract **FileFilter** class and implements the abstract methods.

- **int showDialog(Component parent, String approveButtonText)**

This method shows a file chooser dialog box that lets the user select a file. If the purpose of the dialog is to open or save a file, you might want to use one of the more specific show methods.

- **int showOpenDialog(Component parent)**

This method shows a file chooser dialog box that lets the user select a file to open. The title of the dialog box and the button for selecting a file will say "Open".

- **int showSaveDialog(Component parent)**

This method shows a file chooser dialog box that lets the user select a file to save. The title of the dialog box and the button for approving a file name will say "Save".

JFrame Class

The **JFrame** class inherits from **java.awt.Frame** and is used in a similar way. One important difference, though, is that components are not added directly to a **JFrame** as they are to a **Frame**. Instead, all components except menus are added to the content pane of a **JFrame** object.

The content pane can be accessed using the **getContentPane** method, and can be set using the **setContentPane** method. A **JPanel** or similar container can be set as the content pane. The default content pane of a **JFrame** will use the **BorderLayout** manager.

By default, a **JFrame** will close when the user clicks on the close button. However, if the frame is the main window of an application, you will want to set the default close operation (using the **setDefaultCloseOperation** method) to **EXIT_ON_CLOSE** so that the program will exit when the user closes the frame.

The **ColorPanel** example in the **Complete Examples** section shows how to use the content panel of a **JFrame** as well as the border layout and the default close operation.

Constants

```
static final int EXIT_ON_CLOSE
```

Used with the **setDefaultCloseOperation** to specify what will happen when the user closes the frame. When this value is passed to **setDefaultCloseOperation**, the application will quit when the user closes the frame. Versions of Java prior to 1.3 do not have this value.

Constructors

- `JFrame()`
- `JFrame(String title)`

Methods

- `int getDefaultCloseOperation()`
- `void setDefaultCloseOperation(int operation)`

Determines what will happen when the user closes the frame. Choices for the operation parameter include **EXIT_ON_CLOSE** (defined in JFrame), **HIDE_ON_CLOSE**, **DISPOSE_ON_CLOSE**, and **DO_NOTHING_ON_CLOSE**. The last three constants are defined in the `javax.swing.WindowConstants` interface.

- `void update(Graphics g)`

This method calls `paint(g)`.

- `JMenuBar getJMenuBar()`
- `void setJMenuBar(JMenuBar menubar)`
- `Container getContentPane()`
- `void setContentPane(Container contentPane)`

Components (other than menu bars) are added to the content pane rather than directly to the frame. For example, a button could be added using the following method call:

```
frame.getContentPane().add(myButton);
```

Example   The following code can be used in an application's **main** method to show a frame. The application will exit when the user closes the frame The class **MyFrame** inherits from **JFrame**.

```
MyFrame frame = new MyFrame();
frame.setDefaultCloseOperation(EXIT_ON_CLOSE);
frame.pack();
frame.setVisible(true);
```

JLabel Class

This class inherits from **JComponent** directly, and inherits indirectly from **Container** and **Component**. A label can display a single line of text. You can use the **JTextArea** class, to display more than one line of text. In addition to displaying text, a **JLabel** component can display an icon.

Constructors

- `JLabel()`
- `JLabel(Icon image)`
- `JLabel(Icon image, int horizontalAlignment)`
- `JLabel(String text)`

- `JLabel(String text, Icon icon, int horizontalAlignment)`
- `JLabel(String text, int horizontalAlignment)`

Methods

- `String getText()`
- `void setText(String text)`
- `int getHorizontalAlignment()`
- `void setHorizontalAlignment(int alignment)`
- `int getVerticalAlignment()`
- `void setVerticalAlignment(int alignment)`

The values for horizontal alignment are **LEFT**, **CENTER**, **RIGHT**, **LEADING**, and **TRAILING**. **LEADING** and **TRAILING** are used to make alignment independent of whether the language is left-to-right or right-to-left. The values for vertical alignment are **TOP**, **CENTER**, and **BOTTOM**. The alignment constants are defined in `javax.swing.SwingConstants`.

Example   In this code, `label` is defined as a reference variable for class `JLabel`.

```
label = new JLabel("Hello World");
label.setHorizontalAlignment(SwingConstants.RIGHT);
```

JMenu Class

This class inherits from `JMenuItem` directly, and inherits indirectly from **AbstractButton** and `JComponent`. Because `JMenu` inherits from `JMenuItem`, a menu can be a menu item, which allows submenus.

See the description of the `JMenuBar` class for sample code that creates a menu bar, a menu, and several menu items and then adds the menu bar to a frame.

Constructors

- `JMenu()`
- `JMenu(String s)`
- `JMenu(String s, boolean b)`

The string parameter to the constructors specifies the label for the menu. The `boolean` parameter specifies whether or not the menu is a tear-off menu.

Methods

- `JMenuItem add(JMenuItem menuItem)`
- `JMenuItem add(String s)`
- `void addSeparator()`

These methods allow the programmer to add items to a menu. The item added can take the form of a `MenuItem` instance or a `String` object.

A separator is not a menu item that the user can select. Separators provide a way to group related menu items. Usually a separator shows up as a line in the menu.

- **`void insert(String s, int pos)`**
- **`JMenuItem insert(JMenuItem menuItem, int pos)`**
- **`void insertSeparator(int index)`**

These methods provide alternative ways to add items to a menu at a certain position in the menu.

- **`JMenuItem getItem(int pos)`**
- **`int getItemCount()`**

- **`boolean isTearOff()`**

Returns **true** if the menu is a tear-off menu.

- **`void remove(JMenuItem item)`**
- **`void remove(int pos)`**
- **`void removeAll()`**

JMenuBar Class

A **`JMenuBar`** instance is a component that can be used to display menus in a frame or a dialog. Although most Swing components are added to the content pane of a frame, a menu bar is added directly to the frame. Sample code that uses **`JMenuBar`** (as well as **`JMenu`** and **`JMenuItem`**) follows the method descriptions.

Constructors

- **`JMenuBar()`**

Methods

- **`JMenu add(JMenu menu)`**

This method adds a menu to the menu bar.

- **`JMenu getMenu(int index)`**

This method retrieves a menu from the menu bar. The **index** parameter specifies which menu to return. The index of a menu will be zero for the first menu added, 1 for the second, and so on.

- **`int getMenuCount()`**

You can use this method to find out how many menus have been added to the menu bar.

Example   In the following code, **MyFrame** extends **JFrame** and implements **ActionListener**. This code is in the **main** method of an application.

The code creates a menu bar, adds one menu labeled "Pie," and adds three menu items. The **actionPerformed** method in **MyFrame** is not shown here, but it uses the **getActionCommand** method from **ActionEvent** to find out which menu item was selected.

```
MyFrame frame = new MyFrame();
JMenuBar menuBar = new JMenuBar();
JMenu menu = new JMenu("Pie");
JMenuItem item;
```

```
menuBar.add(menu);

item = new JMenuItem("Cherry");
item.addActionListener(frame);
menu.add(item);

item = new JMenuItem("Peach");
item.addActionListener(frame);
menu.add(item);

menu.addSeparator();

item = new JMenuItem("Banana Cream");
item.addActionListener(frame);
menu.add(item);

frame.setJMenuBar(menuBar);
```

JMenuItem Class

This class is used to create menu items that can be added to a menu in a menu bar or a pop-up menu. **JMenuItem** extends **AbstractButton**, so menu items have much in common with buttons. In particular, both can be used with action listeners.

See the description of the **JMenuBar** class for an example of how to add menu items to a menu in a menu bar.

Constructors

- **JMenuItem(Icon icon)**
- **JMenuItem(String text)**
- **JMenuItem(String text, Icon icon)**

These constructors can create menu items that have an icon, text, or both text and an icon.

Methods

- **void setEnabled(boolean isEnabled)**

If **isEnabled** is **false**, the menu item will be disabled and the user will not be able to select that item. If it is **true**, the menu item will be enabled and can be selected.

This class inherits the following method from **AbstractButton**:

- **void addActionListener(ActionListener listener)**

JOptionPane Class

This class provides an easy way to make several standard types of modal dialogs, including message dialogs, confirm dialogs, and input dialogs. The standard dialogs include an icon, a message, and option buttons. Some include an input component (other than buttons).

The easiest way to use this class is to call one of the four static methods **showMessageDialog**, **showConfirmDialog**, **showInputDialog**, or **showOptionDialog** (referred to below as **show_____Dialog** methods). This description focuses on the use of these static methods rather than using the constructors for the class.

The icon displayed depends on the type of dialog, the `messageType` parameter (if there is one), and the current look-and-feel. The standard types of icons are error, information, question, and warning. Specifying a **messageType** of `PLAIN_MESSAGE` will produce a dialog box that does not have an icon. Some methods have an `icon` parameter which can be used to specify a custom icon.

The message is text that is displayed in the dialog box. There are three different ways to set the message for a dialog box: as a parameter to the constructor, as a parameter to a `show_____Dialog` method, or using the `setMessage` method. Message parameters are shown as class `Object` but are usually strings.

Option buttons are the buttons on the dialog box that allow the user to respond to a message. As with the message type, there are several ways to set the option type. It can be specified as a parameter to the constructor, as a parameter to a `show_____Dialog` method, or by a method for just that purpose (called `setOptionType`). Each option type constant specifies a set of buttons, with constants for the following:

- the default buttons for the type of dialog
- **Yes** and **No** buttons
- **Yes**, **No**, and **Cancel** buttons
- **OK** and **Cancel** buttons

The exact words on the buttons depend on the look-and-feel in use. The `showOption-Dialog` allows the programmer to specify the text for the buttons.

The methods `showInputDialog` and `showOptionDialog` allow the programmer to specify a list of possibilities from which the user can select. The possibilities are displayed to the user as buttons or in a combo box (or other component) that allows the user to select a value from a list of possible values.

Constants   The following values are used to specify the style of the message displayed in the dialog box. When you use a `show_____Dialog` method, you can specify the message style you want, and this will determine which icon is displayed. Note that different look-and-feels have different icons. The `PLAIN_MESSAGE` style does not have an icon. The parameters that use these values are called `messageType` in the method descriptions below.

- `static int ERROR_MESSAGE`
- `static int INFORMATION_MESSAGE`
- `static int PLAIN_MESSAGE`
- `static int QUESTION_MESSAGE`
- `static int WARNING_MESSAGE`

These values are used to specify the option buttons that appear on the bottom of a confirm dialog box. In the method descriptions shown below, the parameter that uses these values is called `optionType`.

- `static int DEFAULT_OPTION`
- `static int YES_NO_OPTION`
- `static int YES_NO_CANCEL_OPTION`
- `static int OK_CANCEL_OPTION`

These values are returned to indicate which button (or which option) the user clicked.

- `static int CANCEL_OPTION`
- `static int CLOSED_OPTION`

Indicates that the user closed the dialog box without selecting an option.

- `static int NO_OPTION`
- `static int OK_OPTION`
- `static int YES_OPTION`

Methods

- `static void showMessageDialog(Component parentComponent,`
  `                              Object message)`
- `static void showMessageDialog(Component parentComponent,`
  `                              Object message, String title,`
  `                              int messageType)`
- `static void showMessageDialog(Component parentComponent,`
  `                              Object message, String title,`
  `                              int messageType, Icon icon)`

Since the `showMessageDialog` method contains only a single button, there is no information to get back from it and the return type is **void**.

- `static int showConfirmDialog(Component parentComponent,`
  `                             Object message, String title,`
  `                             int optionType, int messageType,`
  `                             Icon icon)`

There are other versions of **showConfirmDialog** that do not require all of the parameters listed above. The buttons that appear in the dialog box depend on the **optionType** parameter, which should be one of the constants **DEFAULT_OPTION**, **YES_NO_OPTION**, **YES_NO_CANCEL_OPTION**, or **OK_CANCEL_OPTION**. The returned value tells which button was pressed. You can compare the return value to the constants **YES_OPTION**, **NO_OPTION**, or **CANCEL_OPTION** to determine which button was pressed.

- `static Object showInputDialog(Component parentComponent,`
  `                              Object message, String title,`
  `                              int messageType, Icon icon,`
  `                              Object[] selectionValues,`
  `                              Object initialSelectionValue)`

There are other versions of **showInputDialog** that do not require all of the parameters listed above. The object that is returned is the one the user selected from **selectionValues**.

- `static int showOptionDialog(Component parentComponent,`
  `                            Object message, String title,`
  `                            int optionType, int messageType,`
  `                            Icon icon, Object[] options,`
  `                            Object initialValue)`

The options can be strings, components, or some other kind of object. Components will be displayed on the dialog. Nonstring objects that are not components will be converted to strings using their **toString** methods.

Example

```
Object[] options = {"alpha", "beta", "gamma", "delta",
"omega"};

int choice = JOptionPane.showOptionDialog(this,
                              "Care for a Greek letter?",
                              "Alphabet Soup",
                              JOptionPane.DEFAULT_OPTION,
                              JOptionPane.QUESTION_MESSAGE,
                              null,
                              options,
                              options[0]);

setLabel(choice + " " + (String) options[choice]);
```

This code is used in a method in a class that extends **JFrame** and includes a **setLabel** method to display text in a label in the frame. The first parameter, **"this"**, passes a reference to the frame as the parent of the dialog box. The second parameter is the message text displayed in the dialog box. The third parameter, **"Alphabet Soup"**, is displayed in the title bar of the dialog box. The option type is set to the default.

Since the message type (fifth parameter) is a question, the question icon for the look-and-feel will be displayed. The icon parameter (sixth parameter) is left null, but a custom icon could be passed instead. The seventh parameter is a list of options, which in this case is an array of strings, although options itself is declared as an array of **Object** instances. The last parameter tells what the default value will be; in this case it is **alpha**.

The user's choice is returned and stored in the variable **choice**. The variable choice and the corresponding string are displayed in a label in the frame by the method **setLabel** (defined in the class but not shown here).

JPanel Class

JPanel is a general-use container. As a container, a **JPanel** object uses a layout manager and can have components added to it. As a component, a **JPanel** can be added to a container such as a frame, an applet, or another panel.

Constructors

- **JPanel()**
- **JPanel(LayoutManager layout)**
- **JPanel(boolean isDoubleBuffered)**
- **JPanel(LayoutManager layout, boolean isDoubleBuffered)**

Methods   The commonly used methods of the **JPanel** class are inherited from **JCompo-nent** or **Container**. Some important methods inherited from **Component** are listed below:

- **Component add(Component comp)**
- **void add(Component comp, Object constraints)**

What kinds of constraints are passed as the second parameter depends on the layout manager of the panel.

- **void setLayout(LayoutManager manager)**

JPasswordField Class

A password field is a text field that does not display the text entered by the user. The password field will show one echo character (***** for example) for each character typed by the user.

The **JPasswordField** class extends **JTextField**, which in turn inherits from **JTextComponent**.

Constructors

- **JPasswordField()**
- **JPasswordField(int columns)**
- **JPasswordField(String text)**
- **JPasswordField(String text, int columns)**

The text parameter specifies the initial text of the password field. The columns parameter specifies how many columns it will have, or in other words, roughly how many characters wide the field will be. The initial text will not be displayed except as a number of echo characters.

Methods

- **char[] getPassword()**

This method returns an array of characters rather than a string. If you need the password to be in string form, you can use a **String** constructor, as follows:

```
System.out.println("the password is " +
                    new String(passField.getPassword()));
```

- **char getEchoChar()**
- **void setEchoChar(char c)**

These methods get or set a character to display in the password field instead of characters actually typed by the user.

Example   The following code is from the constructor of a class that extends **JFrame** and **ActionListener**. **passField** is an instance variable that is class **JPassword-Field**. When the frame is displayed, the password contains six dollar signs, one for each character in the intial text, **"secret"**.

```
passField = new JPasswordField("secret", 10);
passField.setEchoChar('$');
```

```
getContentPane().add(passField);
passField.addActionListener(this);
```

JRadioButton Class

A radio button is like a check box except that check boxes are usually independent of each other, while the status of a radio button depends on the status of other radio buttons in the same group. Only one radio button from a group can be selected at a time, so they are used to display mutually exclusive options.

A **ButtonGroup** object is used to specify which radio buttons are part of a group.

Constructors

- **JRadioButton()**
- **JRadioButton(Icon icon)**
- **JRadioButton(Icon icon, boolean selected)**
- **JRadioButton(String text)**
- **JRadioButton(String text, boolean selected)**
- **JRadioButton(String text, Icon icon)**
- **JRadioButton(String text, Icon icon, boolean selected)**

The constructors allow various combinations of icon, text, and selected status as parameters.

Methods

- **boolean isSelected()**
- **void setSelected(boolean b)**

These two methods are inherited from the **AbstractButton** class and may be used to retrieve or set the state of the check box.

As an instance of a descendant class of **AbstractButton**, a check box can be associated with several kinds of listeners. Listeners are added using the following inherited methods:

- **void addActionListener(ActionListener l)**
- **void addChangeListener(ChangeListener l)**
- **void addItemListener(ItemListener l)**

JScrollPane Class

The **JScrollPane** class provides an easy way to make another component scrollable. For instance, using a **JLabel** with an **IconImage** picture in it, you can make a scrollable picture.

Constructors

- **JScrollPane(Component view)**

The **view** parameter specifies what the user will view in the scroll pane. Since **JComponent** inherits from **Component** (via **Container**), the parameter can be a Swing component.

Methods

- **JScrollBar getVerticalScrollBar()**
- **JScrollBar getHorizontalScrollBar()**

Using the scrollbar objects returned by these methods, you can get and set the scrollbar values.

Example

```
JLabel label;
ImageIcon icon;
JScrollPane scrollPane;

icon = new ImageIcon("lighthouse.jpg");
label = new JLabel(icon);
scrollPane = new JScrollPane(label);
getContentPane().add(scrollPane);
```

Code similar to this was used with a **JFrame** to make a scrollable picture in the frame. The following code, which is also very similar, was used to make a scrollable text area.

```
JScrollPane scrollPane;
JTextArea textArea;

textArea = new JTextArea(10, 30);
scrollPane = new JScrollPane(textArea);
getContentPane().add(scrollPane);
```

In both of these examples, the scrollbars do not show up initially because the viewport is made big enough to show the entire component. However, the scrollbars appear if the frame is resized to be smaller or if longer text lines are entered in the text area.

JTable Class

The **JTable** class can be used to make simple tables that display all information as text, or more complicated tables that use check boxes and combo boxes. You must define a table model in order to make the best use of the fancier table features. A table model is an object that contains the data displayed in the table. The model provides a consistent way to set and get data values even though the display of the table changes.

A table model implements the **javax.swing.table.TableModel** interface, and includes methods for getting the row and column counts, telling which cells are editable, and getting and setting cell values. The table component calls methods in the table model to properly display cell contents and allow the user to edit the cells marked as editable.

To make a table model, you can extend the class **AbstractTableModel** (in the **javax.swing.table** package) and implement the following methods:

```
int getRowCount();
int getColumnCount();
Object getValueAt(int row, int column);
```

One way to implement **getValueAt** would be to include a two-dimensional array in the table model class. Then the parameters passed to the method can be used to index into the array and return the value to be displayed in the **JTable** component.

In addition to the three required methods listed above, the following methods are often useful in a table model:

```
boolean isCellEditable(int rowIndex, int columnIndex)
void setValueAt(Object aValue, int rowIndex, int columnIndex)
```

If you don't want to define a class for the table model, you can use a default table model. The easiest way to do this is to pass a two-dimensional array of data to the **JTable** constructor. Use the **getModel** method of the table to get the model (which will implement the **TableModel** interface), and then use the **getValueAt** and **setValueAt** methods to get and set values in the table. Note that the table component itself has **getValueAt** and **setValueAt** methods, but the column indexes that they use are the indexes of the columns in the order in which they are displayed. Since the user can rearrange the order of the columns, using the display order index could cause errors. Instead, use the table model, where the order of the columns does not change.

Constructors

- **JTable(int numRows, int numColumns)**
This constructor creates a table of empty cells that has **numRow** rows and **numColumns** columns.

- **JTable(Object[][] data, Object[] columnNames)**
This constructor creates a table that uses a default table model and copies the elements of data to the table model. Typically, **columnNames** would be an array of strings.

- **JTable(TableModel model)**
This constructor creates a table to display the data in the table model passed as a parameter.

- **JTable(Vector data, Vector columnNames)**
The **data** parameter is a vector of vectors.

Methods

- **TableModel getModel()**
- **void setModel(TableModel dataModel)**
These two methods get and set the table model of the table. In some cases this will be a default model. The model provides methods that can be used to access data from the table. A brief description of table models is included in the **JTable** description.

The **JTable** class includes numerous methods, most of which are not listed here. Many of the methods use related classes. In fact, there is a package (**javax.swing.table**) just for classes that are used with tables. Using these classes and methods, it is possible to configure tables in many different ways.

Example   This code shows a simple example of using a table in a class that extends **JFrame**. By default, all of the cells will be editable. The resulting table displays two columns, each of which includes a heading and two rows of data. The **println** statement prints out the word **"Snowflake"** when this code is executed.

```
String[] columnNames = {"Name", "Species"};
String[][] tableData =
                {{"Snowflake", "Cat"}, {"Smokey", "Cat"},
                 {"Charm", "Rabbit"}, {"Spin", "Rabbit"}};

JTable table = new JTable(tableData, columnNames);
TableModel model = table.getModel();
JScrollPane scroll = new JScrollPane(table);

getContentPane().setLayout(new BorderLayout());
getContentPane().add(scroll, BorderLayout.CENTER);

String item = (String) model.getValueAt(0,0);
System.out.println(item);
```

JTextArea Class

A text area is a component that can display multiple lines of text. It can be set to allow the user to edit it, or to not allow changes by the user. All of the text in a text area will be the same font and style. If you need multiple fonts and styles in a text component, you can use **JEditorPane** or **JTextPane**.

JTextArea inherits from **JTextComponent**. Among the methods it inherits are methods to manipulate the selected text.

In Swing, text areas do not have built-in scrollbars as they do in the AWT package, so you must use a scroll pane if you want scrollbars.

Constructors

- **JTextArea(String text)**
- **JTextArea(int rows, int columns)**
- **JTextArea(String text, int rows, int columns)**

The constructors for **JTextArea** can specify the initial text, the size in rows and columns, or both.

Methods

- **void setEditable(boolean b)**

This method is inherited from **JTextComponent**. If called with **true** as the parameter, the user will able to edit the text area.

- **void append(String str)**
- **void insert(String str, int pos)**
- **void replaceRange(String str, int start, int end)**

These methods are used to manipulate the text in a text area. The parameters **pos**, **start**, and **end** are all offsets into the text, given in number of characters. The **replaceRange** method may be used to delete text by passing null or an empty string as the first parameter.

If you need to manipulate text in terms of lines rather than offsets, you can use the methods shown below to convert from offsets to line numbers and vice versa.

- `int getLineCount()`
- `int getLineOfOffset(int offset) throws BadLocationException`
- `int getLineStartOffset(int line) throws BadLocationException`
- `int getLineEndOffset(int line) throws BadLocationException`

Unless a text area's document model has been set to **null** (using methods not shown here), you can index into it using lines and offsets.

- `Font getFont()`
- `void setFont(Font f)`

These methods get and set the font for the text area. The **getFont** method is inherited. For a **JTextArea**, the font will be the same for all text in the component.

- `boolean getLineWrap()`
- `void setLineWrap(boolean wrap)`
- `void setWrapStyleWord(boolean word)`

These methods get and set the line-wrap property of the text area. If the line wrap is set to true, then you can set the wrap style to wrap at word boundaries (white space) rather than break up a word over two lines.

javax.swing.text.JTextComponent Class

Although this class is in the **javax.swing.text** package rather than **javax.swing**, it is included here to show some of the methods available for use with **JTextArea** and **JTextField**, which inherit from it. This class provides methods for using the system clipboard and programmatically selecting text, among other things.

Methods

- `void copy()`
- `void cut()`
- `void paste()`

These three methods allow the program to work with the system clipboard. The copy and cut operations both put the selected text into the clipboard. The cut operation removes the selected area at the same time, whereas the copy operation does not.

The paste operation pastes text from the clipboard into the component text. The paste operation will replace the contents of the current selection if there is a selection.

- `String getText()`
- `void setText(String t)`
- `String getSelectedText()`

There are two ways to select text in a **JTextComponent**. The caret (or insertion point) position methods select text by first setting the caret position and then moving it. The **select** method specifies the beginning and end positions of the selection. The **select** method is provided for compatibility with AWT text components and is implemented in terms of the caret methods.

- **void moveCaretPosition(int pos)**
- **int getCaretPosition()**
- **void setCaretPosition(int position)**
- **void select(int selectionStart, int selectionEnd)**
- **void selectAll()**
- **void setEditable(boolean b)**

JTextField Class

This class displays a single line of text that may or may not be editable by the user. The **setEditable** method inherited from **JTextComponent** makes the field editable (if its parameter is **true**) or not editable.

Constructors

- **JTextField()**
- **JTextField(int columns)**
- **JTextField(String text)**
- **JTextField(String text, int columns)**

Methods

- **void addActionListener(ActionListener l)**
An action event occurs when the user presses **Enter** in the text field.
- **void removeActionListener(ActionListener l)**
- **int getColumns()**
- **void setColumns(int columns)**
- **protected int getColumnWidth()**
- **int getHorizontalAlignment()**
- **void setHorizontalAlignment(int alignment)**
- **void setActionCommand(String command)**
- **Font getFont()**
- **void setFont(Font f)**
The preceding two methods get and set the font for the text area. The **getFont** method is inherited.

JToggleButton Class

A toggle button has two states, and clicking the button changes from one state to the other. The **JToggleButton** class is the parent of **JCheckBox** and **JRadioButton**, which are the classes used for two specific kinds of toggle buttons. The parent class of **JToggleButton** is **AbstractButton**.

Constructors

- **JToggleButton(Icon icon)**
- **JToggleButton(Icon icon, boolean selected)**
- **JToggleButton(String text)**
- **JToggleButton(String text, boolean selected)**
- **JToggleButton(String text, Icon icon)**
- **JToggleButton(String text, Icon icon, boolean selected)**

Like a **JButton** object, a toggle button can be initialized with an icon, a string, or both. Unlike a **JButton**, a toggle button's initial state can also be specified, using the **selected** parameter to the constructors.

Methods

- **boolean isSelected()**

This method is inherited from **AbstractButton** and can be used to determine which state the button is in, selected or not selected.

- **void setSelected(Boolean state)**

This method is also inherited from **AbstractButton**.

JWindow Class

A window is a container similar to a frame except that it does not have a title bar or window buttons (close, maximize, minimize). As with a **JFrame** instance, components are added to the content pane rather than directly to the window. Likewise, a layout manager should be used with the content pane rather than with the window itself.

This class extends **java.awt.Window**.

Constructors

- **JWindow()**
- **JWindow(Frame owner)**
- **JWindow(Window owner)**

These three constructors allow a window to be created with no specified owner, with a frame owner, or with a window owner. Since **JFrame** extends **Frame,** and **JWindow** extends **Window**, the owner of a window can be a **JFrame** or a **JWindow**.

Methods

- **Container getContentPane()**

Since components are added to the content pane rather than to the window itself, and the window has no close button, there are relatively few methods that are commonly used with windows of this type.

Timer Class

A timer is used to delay for a specified period of time. The timer can be set to fire once when the time expires or repeatedly at specified intervals. When each delay period is over, the timer causes an action event.

The three main characteristics of a timer are the length of the delay, whether it repeats, and whether or not it coalesces messages. The length of the delay is set in milliseconds. The method **setRepeats** takes a boolean argument that tells whether or not the timer repeats. Coalescing messages means to combine multiple messages. It occurs if the timer has expired several times but the messages have been queued because there wasn't time to send them. If there is more than one message, and the coalescing property is set to true, only one message is sent. If the coalescing property is false, and several messages are queued, the queued messages will all be sent with no delay between them.

Constructors

• **Timer(int delay, ActionListener listener)**
The delay is specified in milliseconds (thousandths of seconds). The action listener receives notification of an event when the time expires.

Methods

• **void start()**
• **void stop()**
• **void restart()**
These methods are used to control the timer.

• **boolean isRunning()**
This method returns **true** if the timer is currently running.

• **int getDelay()**
• **void setDelay(int delay)**
• **void setInitialDelay(int initialDelay)**
These methods get and set the interval until the timer fires. The initial delay can have a different length than the later delays.

• **boolean isRepeats()**
• **void setRepeats(boolean flag)**
These methods retrieve or set the **boolean** value that tells whether the timer will repeat.

• **void addActionListener(ActionListener listener)**
• **EventListener[] getListeners(Class listenerType)**
• **void removeActionListener(ActionListener listener)**
These methods add an action listener, get the current list of listeners, and remove a listener.

• **boolean isCoalesce()**
• **void setCoalesce(boolean flag)**
If the coalesce property is set to true, and there is more than one pending message, then only one message will be sent.

CHAPTER 2

Complete Examples

A common approach to programming is to find a program that is similar to the one you want to write, and then modify it and expand it to include the features that the new program should have. Java provides an excellent library of classes (the Java API) that you can use to add functionality to your program, and there are many other sources of Java classes on the Internet, but you need a base to build on before you can start. The examples in this section provide several different bases on which you can build to create the programs you want.

Each example in this section is a small but complete program that you can run. Some are applets, and some are applications. There are three kinds of applications: one (**PageWriter**) uses a text interface with command-line parameters; another (**PictureFrame**) uses a **Frame** and shows how to make the frame close box work. The third application (**ColorPanel**) uses a **JFrame** and shows how to add components (buttons, in this case) to the content pane of the frame. Most of the Java applications you write will go into one of these categories and can be written using one of these examples as a starting point.

The applets in this section include an example of using the original **Applet** class (**ShowDocApplet**), as well as the Swing **JApplet** class (**SpotlightApplet**). The **ShowDoc** applet example demonstrates interaction with the Web browser.

HOW TO RUN APPLICATIONS

The two applications, **PageWriter** and **PictureFrame**, can be typed in using any text editor or the editor of a Java IDE. If you are using the Java SDK, you can compile the program using a command line like this one:

```
javac PageWriter.java
```

where **PageWriter.java** is the source file for the program. The Java compiler expects file names to always end in **.java**, so don't forget that. If there are no error messages from the compiler, it will produce a class file with the same name except that the last part will be **.class** instead of **.java**. If you get error messages from the compiler, you can look at the last section of this manual for help in understanding and fixing the problems.

Once your program compiles, you can run a Java application by typing a command like this one:

```
java PageWriter
```

where **PageWriter** is the name of a class that contains a **main** method. In order for the program to run, **main** must be spelled exactly as shown here (all lower-case letters), and it must be a **public static** method with one argument that is an array of strings. Here is the first line of the main method from the **PageWriter** example:

```
public static void main(String[] args) {
```

HOW TO RUN APPLETS

To run an applet, you need to compile the source file for applications, as shown above. You also need to make an HTML file that includes an APPLET tag. The **HTML Tutorial** section tells how to make that kind of page. After you have made the HTML file, you can use the appletviewer or a Java-enabled browser to see the applet in action. To use the appletviewer, type a command like this:

```
appletviewer spotlight.html
```

where **spotlight.html** is the name of the HTML file that has an APPLET tag for your applet.

Example: PageWriter

This application demonstrates reading and writing from text files, using the classes **FileReader**, **BufferedReader**, **FileWriter**, and **PrintWriter**. It also shows an example of command-line parameters to **main** and the use of the **StringTokenizer** class to get words from a line of the file.

The program generates one HTML file for each line in the file that contains a list of names. For this example, the file of names contains only first and last names (last name first) separated by semicolons.

A program like this one is useful when a Web site has many small files that should be consistent. If the style of the Web page changes, or information must be added, deleted, or changed, then the list of names can be updated and all of the pages can be generated again. Although in this case the information in the text file is just first and last names, the same type of program can be used to include additional information, such as phone, address, or e-mail address.

After compiling the **PageWriter.java** file, you can run the program by typing this at the command prompt:

```
java PageWriter directory.txt
```

where **directory.txt** (or the file name of your choice) is a text file that includes a last name followed by a first name on each line. The two names on each line should be separated by a semicolon.

Code for the PageWriter *Example*

```java
import java.io.*;
import java.util.StringTokenizer;

public class PageWriter {
    public void makePage(String fileName) {
        BufferedReader inFile;
        String inLine;
        try {
            inFile = new BufferedReader(new FileReader
                                            (fileName));
            inLine = inFile.readLine();
            while (inLine != null) {
                writePage(inLine);
                inLine = inFile.readLine();
            }
        }
        catch(Exception e) {
            System.out.println(e.getMessage());
        }
    }

    public void writePage(String pageInfo) {
        StringTokenizer parser = new StringTokenizer
                                        (pageInfo, ";");
        String lastName = parser.nextToken();
        String fileName = lastName + ".html";
        String firstName = parser.nextToken();

        try {
            PrintWriter outFile =
                    new PrintWriter(new FileWriter(fileName));
            outFile.println("<HTML>");
            outFile.println("<CENTER><H1>" + firstName + " "
                                + lastName + "</CENTER></H1>");
            outFile.println("</HTML>");
            outFile.close();
        }
        catch (Exception e) {
            System.out.println(e.getMessage());
        }
    }

    public static void main(String[] args) {
        PageWriter writer = new PageWriter();
        writer.makePage(args[0]);
    }
}
```

Example: `PictureFrame`

The `PictureFrame` application demonstrates an application that uses a **Frame** object for its interface. It demonstrates how to make a working close box on a frame, and also demonstrates how to use a pop-up menu and a file dialog. The pop-up menu works only with the right mouse button, which is the convention with multibutton mice.

The `PictureFrame` class inherits from **Frame** and implements three listener interfaces: one for window events so that the close box will work closely, one for mouse events so that the pop-up menu will work correctly, and the third for action events, which is also used with the pop-up menu. The program does not use several of the mouse listener and window listener methods, but they must all be defined or the class will not implement the interfaces and will not compile.

The program displays the pop-up menu when the **mousePressed** listener method is called. Each item in the pop-up menu is associated with an action listener (the **Picture Frame** object, in this case), so that an action event occurs when the user selects a menu item, and the correct action for the menu selection will be done.

The pop-up menu includes two items. Change Picture opens a file dialog so that the user can select a new picture to display. When the new picture is displayed, the program adjusts the size of the frame to match the dimensions of the picture. Exit closes the frame and quits the program.

Code for the `PictureFrame` Example

```java
import java.awt.*;
import java.awt.event.*;

class PictureFrame extends Frame implements WindowListener,
                        MouseListener, ActionListener {
    private PopupMenu pop;
    private MenuItem item;
    private Image picture;
    private FileDialog fileSelect;

    public PictureFrame () {
        addWindowListener(this);
        addMouseListener(this);

        pop = new PopupMenu();
        item = new MenuItem("Change Picture");
        item.addActionListener(this);
        pop.add(item);
        item = new MenuItem("Exit");
        item.addActionListener(this);
        pop.add(item);
        add(pop);
    }
```

```java
public void paint(Graphics g) {
    if (picture != null) {
        g.drawImage(picture, 0, 0, this);
        adjust();
    }
}

public void setPicture(String imgFileName) {
  picture = Toolkit.getDefaultToolkit().getImage
                                      (imgFileName);
}

private void changePicture() {
    fileSelect = new FileDialog(this,
                "Select a picture file", FileDialog.LOAD);
    fileSelect.show();
    setPicture(fileSelect.getDirectory() +
                        fileSelect.getFile());
    adjust();
}

private void adjust() {
    int imgWidth = picture.getWidth(this);
    int imgHeight = picture.getHeight(this);
    if (imgWidth > 0 && imgHeight > 0) {
        setSize(imgWidth, imgHeight);
    }
}

private void quit() {
    System.exit(0);
}

public void actionPerformed(ActionEvent e) {
    if (e.getActionCommand().equals("Exit")) {
        quit();
    } else if (e.getActionCommand().equals
                        ("Change Picture")) {
        changePicture();
    }
}

public void windowOpened(WindowEvent e) {}
public void windowClosed(WindowEvent e) {}
public void windowIconified(WindowEvent e) {}
public void windowDeiconified(WindowEvent e) {}
public void windowActivated(WindowEvent e) {}
public void windowDeactivated(WindowEvent e) {}

public void windowClosing(WindowEvent e) {
  quit();
}
```

```
public void mouseClicked(MouseEvent e) {}
public void mouseEntered(MouseEvent e) {}
public void mouseExited(MouseEvent e) {}
public void mouseReleased(MouseEvent e) {}

public void mousePressed(MouseEvent e) {
    // ONLY SHOW THE POP-UP MENU IF THE RIGHT BUTTON IS
    CLICKED
    if ((e.getModifiers() & InputEvent.BUTTON3_MASK)
            == InputEvent.BUTTON3_MASK) {
      pop.show(e.getComponent(), e.getX(), e.getY());
    }
}

public static void main(String[] args) {
  PictureFrame frame = new PictureFrame();
  frame.setSize(300, 200);
    if (args.length == 1) {
        frame.setPicture(args[0]);
    }
  frame.show();
}
}
```

Example: `ShowDocApplet`

This applet demonstrates how to use the **AppletContext** interface and the **URL** class. When the user clicks on one of the buttons, the Web browser will display the URL associated with that button in a different window than the one in which the applet is running. For this applet to work correctly, you must run it in a Java-enabled browser, rather than with the appletviewer.

Code for the `ShowDocApplet` Example

```
import java.applet.*;
import java.awt.*;
import java.awt.event.*;
import java.net.URL;

public class ShowDocApplet extends Applet implements
                                    ActionListener {
  private Button showButton, show2Button;

  public void init() {
     showButton = new Button("Show");
     add(showButton);
     showButton.addActionListener(this);

     show2Button = new Button("Show Too");
     add(show2Button);
     show2Button.addActionListener(this);
  }
```

```
public void actionPerformed(ActionEvent evt) {
    try {
        if (evt.getActionCommand() == "Show") {
            URL showURL = new URL(getDocumentBase(),
                                  "show.html");
            getAppletContext().showDocument(showURL,
                                        "show window");
        } else {
            URL showURL = new URL(getDocumentBase(),
                                  "show2.html");
            getAppletContext().showDocument(showURL,
                                        "show window");
        }
    }
    catch (Exception e) {
        System.out.println("Exception");
    }
}
}
```

Example: `SpotlightApplet`

This applet demonstrates how to use the `JApplet` class. Note that the `JButton` component is added to the content pane rather than to the applet itself. Applets have easy access to bitmap images in their document base, and this example shows how to use that capability. It also demonstrates the use of a clipping area, and shows how a `KeyListener` can be used to make a program respond to key presses without reading text.

The applet shows a dark rectangle with a circle showing the picture underneath. When the user presses the arrow keys, the circle moves, giving a spotlight or searchlight effect. When the user pushes the button labeled "Push Me," the program toggles the searchlight effect. The first time the user presses the button, the searchlight goes off and the entire picture is displayed. The next time the user pushes the button, the searchlight effect goes on again, and so on.

For this applet to work correctly, a JPEG image file called "night.jpg" must be in the document base of the applet or the name of the file in the program must be changed. A good exercise you may want to try is changing the applet so that it gets the name of the image file as a parameter from the HTML file.

Code for the `SpotlightApplet` Example

`SpotlightApplet.java`

```java
import java.awt.BorderLayout;
import java.awt.event.*;
import javax.swing.JApplet;
import javax.swing.JButton;

public class SpotlightApplet extends JApplet implements
                                        ActionListener {
    private JButton showButton;
    private boolean useClip;
    SpotlightPanel panel;
```

```java
        public void init() {
            panel = new SpotlightPanel();
            panel.setPic(getImage(getDocumentBase(), "night.jpg"));
            getContentPane().add(panel, BorderLayout.CENTER);

            showButton = new JButton("Push Me");
            showButton.addActionListener(this);
            getContentPane().add(showButton, BorderLayout.SOUTH);

            addKeyListener(panel);
        }

        public void actionPerformed(ActionEvent evt) {
            panel.toggleSpot();
            panel.repaint();
        }
    }
```

SpotlightPanel.java

```java
    import java.awt.*;
    import java.awt.event.*;
    import java.awt.geom.*;
    import javax.swing.JPanel;
public class SpotlightPanel extends JPanel implements KeyListener {
        private static final int INC = 10;
        private static final int CLIP_WIDTH = 100,
                                          CLIP_HEIGHT = 100;

        private int clipX, clipY, clipHeight, clipWidth;
        private Image picture;
        private Shape clip;
        private int width, height;

        private boolean useClip;

        public SpotlightPanel() {
            clipX = 0;
            clipY = 0;
            setBackground(new Color(20, 2, 60));
            useClip = true;
        }

        public void setPic(Image img) {
            picture = img;
        }

        public void toggleSpot() {
            if (useClip) {
               useClip = false;
            } else {
               useClip = true;
            }
        }
```

```java
public void paintComponent(Graphics g) {
   super.paintComponent(g);
   if (useClip) {
      clip = new Ellipse2D.Double(clipX, clipY,
                           CLIP_WIDTH, CLIP_HEIGHT);
      g.setClip(clip);
   }
   g.drawImage(picture, 0, 0, this);
}

public void keyTyped(KeyEvent evt) {
}

public void keyPressed(KeyEvent evt) {
}

public void keyReleased(KeyEvent evt) {
   switch (evt.getKeyCode()) {
   case KeyEvent.VK_UP:
      clipY = clipY - INC > 0 ? clipY - INC : 0;
      break;
   case KeyEvent.VK_DOWN:
      clipY = clipY + INC < getHeight() - CLIP_HEIGHT ?
                     clipY + INC : getHeight() - CLIP_HEIGHT;
      break;

   case KeyEvent.VK_LEFT:
      clipX = clipX - INC > 0 ? clipX - INC : 0;
      break;

   case KeyEvent.VK_RIGHT:
      clipX = clipX + INC < getWidth() - CLIP_WIDTH ?
                     clipX + INC : getWidth() - CLIP_WIDTH;
      break;
   }
   repaint();
   }
}
```

Example: `ColorPanel`

This application shows how to use a **JFrame**. Components, such as the buttons and panel in this example, are added to the content pane rather than to the frame itself. A **JFrame** content pane uses the **BorderLayout** layout manager by default. The buttons are added to the **NORTH**, **SOUTH**, **EAST**, and **WEST** regions of the content frame, and a **JPanel** is added to the **CENTER**. Other Swing components could in turn be added to the **JPanel**.

Code for the `ColorPanel` *Example*

```java
import javax.swing.*;
import java.awt.*;
import java.awt.event.*;

public class ColorPanel extends JFrame implements
                                      ActionListener {
    JButton redButton, blueButton, yellowButton, greenButton;
    JPanel panel;

    public ColorPanel() {
     redButton = new JButton("Red");
     blueButton = new JButton("Blue");
     greenButton = new JButton("Green");
     yellowButton = new JButton("Yellow");
     panel = new JPanel();

     redButton.addActionListener(this);
     blueButton.addActionListener(this);
     greenButton.addActionListener(this);
     yellowButton.addActionListener(this);

     getContentPane().add(redButton, BorderLayout.SOUTH);
     getContentPane().add(blueButton, BorderLayout.NORTH);
     getContentPane().add(greenButton, BorderLayout.EAST);
     getContentPane().add(yellowButton, BorderLayout.WEST);
     getContentPane().add(panel, BorderLayout.CENTER);
    }

    public void actionPerformed(ActionEvent e) {
     if (e.getActionCommand() == "Red") {
        panel.setBackground(Color.red);
     } else if (e.getActionCommand() == "Blue") {
        panel.setBackground(Color.blue);
     } else if (e.getActionCommand() == "Green") {
        panel.setBackground(Color.green);
     } else if (e.getActionCommand() == "Yellow") {
        panel.setBackground(Color.yellow);
     }
    }

    public static void main(String[] args) {
     ColorPanel frame = new ColorPanel();
     frame.setDefaultCloseOperation(EXIT_ON_CLOSE);
     frame.pack();
     frame.setSize(300, 200);
     frame.setVisible(true);
    }
}
```

Example: WordCount

This program counts the number of times that different words appear in a file. The file it reads is named by a command-line parameter. For example, you could use a command line like this one to count the occurrences of words in a file called **words.txt**:

```
java WordCount words.txt
```

Here is part of the output when the program is run on the first paragraph of this section:

```
Words sorted alphabetically:
a : 4
appear : 1
by : 1
called : 1
command : 2
... some words removed ...
Words sorted by frequency:
a : 4
file : 3
the : 3
command : 2
... some more words removed ...
```

This application uses several parts of the Java collections framework and also demonstrates several new features added to Java in version 1.5.

The program accesses the command-line parameter by using the array of **String** objects passed in as a parameter to **main**. It opens the file and uses a loop to read the lines from the file. For each line, it makes a **StringTokenizer** object to break up the line into words. It then calls a method to trim all the characters but letters from the beginning and end of the string. Another method converts the trimmed string to lower case.

To keep track of the words, the program adds each word it finds to a map. The map associates each word with a count of its occurrences, which is an **Integer** object. If the words were not converted to lower case, then **The** (with a capital **T**) would be considered a different word from **the** (with a lower-case **T**).

When the program encounters a word that is already in the map, it does not add the word, but instead just adds 1 to the count associated with that word.

After all the words from the file have been counted, the **keySet** method of the **Map** interface returns a set of all the keys (in this case, words) stored in the map. It then copies the keys and counts to a list so that they can easily be sorted. Elements of the list are instances of the **Entry** nested class.

The loop that adds the **Entry** objects to the list is a **for** loop that was added to Java in version 1.5. The variable **w** refers to each object in **words** in turn. In this case the **for** loop is used with a set, but it can also be used with other kinds of collections, like lists.

This program uses the generic type mechanism introduced in version 1.5. The **map** variable refers to an object of class **HashMap<String, Integer>**. The names in angle brackets are type parameters. In this case, there are two type parameters, **String** and **Integer**. They indicate that the mapping is from **String** to **Integer**. In other words, each **String** in the map is a key associated with an **Integer**. The **String** key is a word from the file, and the **Integer** associated with that key tells how many times the word appears in the file. Other places where type parameters are used are in the nested classes **FrequencyComparator** and **Entry**, and in the declaration of the **list** variable.

Another feature introduced in 1.5 is called *autoboxing* and *auto-unboxing*. This feature provides a way to copy from a wrapper class to a primitive type, and vice versa, without explicitly calling conversion methods. For an example of auto-unboxing, consider the following line from **WordCount**:

```
count = map.get(word);
```

The **count** variable is type **int**, and the **map.get** method returns an object of class **Integer**. Prior to version 1.5, the **intValue** method of **Integer** would have been used here, but with auto-unboxing no explicit call to **intValue** is needed.

The **WordCount** program sorts the list of words and counts two different times. Both times they are sorted by a **sort** method from the **Collections** class. The first time they are sorted using the **compareTo** method of the **Entry** class, which compares the **word** variables of the **Entry** objects and sorts the entries alphabetically. In this case, the only parameter to **sort** is the collection being sorted.

The second time they are sorted by the **compare** method in the **Frequency-Comparator** class, which compares the **count** variables associated with each word and sorts them by how many times they occur. This time there are two parameters to the **sort** function: the collection to be sorted (which is **list** in this case) and a comparator object.

The statements that print the entries use the **printf** method that was added in version 1.5 of Java. The **printf** method is similar to the **printf** function in the C programming language. Its first parameter is a format string that tells how to print the remaining parameters. The format string **"%s : %d\n"** tells the method that the next parameter should be printed as a string, and the following parameter as a decimal number. The spaces, colon, and newline characters are literals that will be printed the same way every time the statement executes.

Code for the WordCount *Example*

```java
import java.io.*;
import java.util.*;
public class WordCount {
    static class FrequencyComparator
                            implements Comparator<Entry> {
        public int compare(Entry e1, Entry e2) {
            if (e1.count < e2.count) {
                return 1;
            } else if (e1.count > e2.count) {
                return -1;
```

```
            } else {
                return 0;
            }
        }
    }  // end of FrequencyComparator class

    static class Entry implements Comparable<Entry> {
        private String word;
        private int count;

        public Entry(String w, int c) {
            word = w;
            count = c;
        }

        public int compareTo(Entry e) {
            return word.compareTo(e.word);
        }
    }  // end of Entry class

    public static void main(String args[]) {
        BufferedReader inFile;
        String inLine;
        String fileName = args[0];
        StringTokenizer tokenizer;
        String word;
        int count;
        Map<String, Integer> map
                = new HashMap<String, Integer>();

        try {
            inFile = new BufferedReader(
                    new FileReader(fileName));
            inLine = inFile.readLine();
            while (inLine != null) {
                tokenizer = new StringTokenizer(inLine);
                while (tokenizer.hasMoreTokens()) {
                    word = trimNonLetters(
                            tokenizer.nextToken())
                                .toLowerCase();
                    if (map.containsKey(word)) {
                        count = map.get(word);
                        map.put(word, count + 1);
                    } else {
                        map.put(word, 1);
                    }
                }
                inLine = inFile.readLine();
            }
        }
```

```java
            catch (Exception e) {
                System.out.println(e.getMessage());
            }

            Set<String> words = map.keySet();
            List<Entry> list = new ArrayList<Entry>(words.size());

            for (String w : words) {
                list.add(new Entry(w, map.get(w)));
            }

            Collections.sort(list);

            System.out.print("Words sorted alphabetically:\n");
            for (Entry e : list) {
                System.out.printf("%s : %d\n", e.word, e.count);
            }

            Collections.sort(list, new FrequencyComparator());

            System.out.print("Words sorted by frequency:\n");
            for (Entry e : list) {
                System.out.printf("%s : %d\n", e.word, e.count);
            }
        }   // end of main method

        private static String trimNonLetters(String str) {
            StringBuffer buff = new StringBuffer(str);
            int i;

            while (buff.length() >= 1
                    && !Character.isLetter(buff.charAt(0))) {
                buff.deleteCharAt(0);
            }

            i = buff.length() - 1;
            while (buff.length() > 0 && i >= 0
                    && !Character.isLetter(buff.charAt(i))) {
                buff.deleteCharAt(i);
                i--;
            }
            return new String(buff);
        } // end of trimNonLetters method
} // end of WordCount class
```

An HTML Tutorial

WHAT MAKES A GOOD WEB PAGE?

One day you find yourself the proud owner of a new Web site. The world is waiting for what you have to offer. Now the question is, how can you best present your material on the Web? To answer this question you need to know what makes some Web pages better than others. Naturally there are many opinions on the subject, but here are a few ideas to consider.

First of all, do you know what you want to show? Have you gathered and organized your material? Web surfers soon tire of pages that are all fluff and no content. Put yourself in the place of the reader and think about what they will want and expect to find on your pages, and then put it there.

For the first example in this tutorial, let's suppose that you want to make a home page for yourself. The content for your site includes a picture of yourself, a photo album, your resume, a link to a club you belong to at school, and a fan page about your favorite author.

Content is important and possibly the most important part of a Web page. No matter how good the content is, however, readers will soon be on their way elsewhere if it's convoluted and hard to follow. Just as with a paper, a book, or a speech, organization is important. Not only is the organization on a single page important, but so is navigation—moving from one Web page to another. You'll want to make it as easy as possible for readers to find their way around your site. Think of your home page as the table of contents for your site. It may not provide a lot of information, but if readers can see at a glance what's there, it will help them easily get to the information they want to see.

Always remember that Web pages have to be downloaded to another computer to be read. Long download times will discourage and frustrate readers. In some cases there will be nothing you can do to reduce download time, but you can always warn the reader if following a link will require heavy-duty download time. Another good idea is to keep your home page simple enough to download quickly. That way the reader can see what your page has to offer and can decide whether to take the time to download items on your page.

In our home page example, most of the content will not be on the first page the reader sees. The resume, photo album, and author fan page will be on separate pages with links to them on the main page.

Most likely you are not a graphic designer, but you can still make some great pages if you pay attention to how they look. A simple design is likely to be better than a cluttered and complicated one. On the other hand, simplicity doesn't mean boring or lack of style. Experiment. Search the Web for good designs, and learn from both good and bad designs.

Even though you don't yet know the mechanics of HTML pages, you can sketch several designs for the home page example and get an idea of the advantages and disadvantages of each design. You may want to select a theme for your page. For instance, a scuba diver's home page might use ocean pictures and colors.

Another factor in Web page design is the wide array of browsers in use. Although standards have been written for HTML browsers, there are still some differences in the capabilities of various programs. Sticking to basics improves the chances of your page working even if the reader is using an antiquated browser. Some bells and whistles available for Web pages will only work on one or the other of the two most commonly used browsers, but most basic page components will work equally well in either browser.

In our home page example, we will stick to basic elements that work with any Web browser on the planet: formatted text, pictures, and links. This way we will know that every reader can get at least some information from the page.

Finally, a good Web page does not use the work of others without permission. When permission is given, give credit. Also, let others know if you are willing to share any or all of the materials on your site. Keep in mind that when people talk about the "world-wide" Web, they mean it quite literally. Anyone in the world who has access to the Internet can view your Web site, so respect the privacy of others.

Suppose that you have decided to use an ocean picture as the background for your home page. If you find one that you like on the Web, and find out that it may copied for your own use, you should include a credit somewhere on the page, perhaps at the bottom. The statement giving credit doesn't have to be in large neon letters; even fine print (if still legible) will do the job.

Once you have some content in mind, and have an idea of what makes a good Web site, you're ready to start, but you will need a Web site and some tools before you can put your site together.

TOOLS

The bare minimum for tools is a text editor and a Web browser. You'll need the text editor to make the Web pages, and you'll need a browser to see the result. To view the pages you create, your Web browser doesn't need to be connected to the Internet, but to put your pages on the Web you will need an Internet connection and an account on a Web server.

Just about any text editor will work for making HTML pages, including Simple-Text on a Macintosh and Notepad on a Windows machine. There are also free and low-cost editors available for download from the Internet. Find one that you're comfortable with.

You may find that you prefer working with something a little smarter than a text editor. There are programs available that are specifically designed for editing HTML files, including some free ones like Netscape Composer and Microsoft FrontPage Express (usually installed with Windows). These are WYSIWYG (What You See Is What You Get) editors that show you what the page will look like as you make each change. HTML editors are convenient, but a text editor can give you more control, so the choice is a trade-off between ease of use and flexibility.

In addition to HTML editors, there are other programs that can generate HTML pages, including word processors, presentation software, and spreadsheets. Many of these applications include an option to save the file as HTML. The trade-off here is between ease of use and complexity of the file, since many of these programs generate HTML that is much more complicated than what a person would write with a text editor. Also, HTML doesn't include all of the formatting options that many word processors provide, so your page will probably not look the same after you convert it to HTML.

For the purposes of this tutorial, let's assume that you are using a text editor. That's a good way to begin, because if you later decide to use an HTML editor or a page generator, you will have a better idea of what it's doing and can edit the output if you'd like to.

PUBLISHING WEB PAGES

After you create a Web page, you need to publish it by copying it to a Web server. A Web server is a computer that waits for requests for pages and then gives back (or "serves") the requested file. Since requests for Web pages come over the Internet, a Web server must have an Internet connection.

Many Internet Service Providers (ISPs) allow customers a certain amount of space on a Web server. If you have that kind of account with an ISP, then you have a Web site waiting to be put to use. Your ISP will tell you how much space you are allowed and how to access your space on the server. The most common way to copy files to a Web server is using FTP (which stands for "File Transfer Protocol"). There's a good chance that your computer already has an FTP program on it, and if it doesn't, there are many choices available.

To use FTP, you will need know the name of the Web server, your user name, and the password. Web servers often have names like "www.something.com" or, for students and teachers, "www.something.edu." Read the instructions for your FTP program to find out how to connect to the server and how to copy files to it. FTP programs that use text commands usually have a `put` command to copy files to the server. Many FTP programs have a GUI (Graphic User Interface) where you can copy files by using the mouse to drag and drop icons.

Your ISP can also tell you how to access your Web site with a browser. Often you can type a URL like **`http://www.something.com/username/mypage.html`** into your Web browser to bring up the file **`mypage.html`** from your Web site.

BASICS

Now that you know what content you want on your page, and have an idea for the design, you're ready to start writing HTML. Fire up your text editor and we'll get started. Use the file name `index.html` for the first file you make.

The first thing you need to understand is the concept of *tags*. An HTML tag is enclosed in angle brackets like these: `<>`. The first tag to add to your file is `<HTML>`. Type it in at the beginning of the file and then press enter (or return). The `<HTML>` tag tells the Web browser that the file contains HTML rather than plain text or some other format of information.

Many tags in HTML come in pairs, with an opening tag and a closing tag. A closing tag is usually the same as the opening tag except that it has a slash after the opening angle bracket. The `<HTML>` tag has a matching closing tag, `</HTML>`.

In your text editor, type enter again to leave a blank line, and then type in `</HTML>`, which will be the last thing in the file. Everything in the file will go between the opening HTML tag and the closing HTML tag.

Now you're almost ready for the first preview of your page. Type your name on the line between the two HTML tags. Your file should now look like this:

```
<HTML>
Marvin Somebody
</HTML>
```

Save the file and start up your Web browser. Open the `index.html` file that you just made. You'll have to navigate through some menus (probably including the File menu) and dialog boxes to open it, but you don't need an Internet connection to open a page that's on your own computer.

When you open your file in the browser, you should see your name on a page with nothing else on it. If you don't see your name, or if you see something else on the page with it, go back to the text editor and carefully check your file to be sure that it looks like the example above. Keep in mind that punctuation can be important, especially the `<` and `>` used for tags.

Now try some text formatting. You can enclose your name in `<H1>` and `</H1>` tags to make it a first-level heading: bigger and bolder. `<H1>` is the biggest heading, but there are also `<H2>`, `<H3>`, and other headings that you can use.

To put more text on your page, use paragraph tags: `<P>` to open and `</P>` to close. The closing tag, `</P>` is often left off, but to keep your pages clean you'll want to put it in. At this point your page will look something like this:

```
<HTML>
 <H1>Marvin Somebody</H1>
 <P>Welcome to my home page.
 I hope you enjoy your visit.
 </P>
</HTML>
```

Try it out in the browser. You'll notice that if you make your browser window wider or narrower, the browser reformats the text to fit. When the browser reformats, it sometimes puts two lines together that aren't together in the HTML, or splits a single line in the HTML to make parts of two lines in the formatted text. This kind of reformatting is one of the main features of HTML, so you'll want to make sure you understand how the browser does it.

Images

Ready to put a picture on your page? It's easy to do, but some of the work needs to be done before you make any changes to the HTML. Make sure that the picture is in a format that Web browsers can use. These formats include JPEG (or JPG) and PNG pictures. Browsers can also use GIF files, but because of intellectual property issues you might want to avoid them.

There are many programs—commercial, shareware, and free—that allow you to convert images from one format to another. Many of these programs also allow you to edit pictures by cropping them, scaling them, changing contrast and brightness, and so on.

One thing to watch with JPEG files is the compression level. Image-processing software will usually let you choose high compression for a smaller file but less quality, and low compression for better quality but a bigger file. Keep in mind that even the lowest level of compression with JPEG will reduce the quality of the image slightly. Every time you open a JPEG image and then save it, the image changes slightly from the original. This means that if you're planning to do a lot of editing with a picture, you should save it in some other format and convert it to JPEG after all the editing is done.

When you decide to put a picture on your page, you're looking at a trade-off between size of the file versus quality and size of the image on the screen. If you use a large file to put a big, high-quality picture on your page, some readers will not wait for it to download. On the other hand, if the picture quality is too low, readers will not bother to look at it. Try out various possibilities to get a good balance between quality and download time.

Go ahead and choose a picture to put on your page. There are many sources for pictures, including drawing and paint programs, scanners, digital cameras, clip art collections, Web sites, and photo disks from film processors. Once you have the file, put it in the same directory that your HTML file is in. Then you can use the **IMAGE** tag to include the picture on your page. The most important attribute of the **IMAGE** tag is the **SOURCE** attribute, which tells the file name (or URL) of the picture. For example, you could include the following tag in your page if you had a JPEG file called **me.jpg** in the same directory as your HTML page:

```
<IMG SRC="me.jpg">
```

The quotes are not necessary, but they don't hurt, and in some cases might avoid problems. Note that **IMG** stands for "image" and can be written out as **IMAGE**, but it's almost always abbreviated to **IMG**. Likewise, **SOURCE** is often abbreviated to **SRC**.

Images don't have to be in the same directory as the HTML file; you can specify a path instead of a simple file name if you'd like.

After adding an image tag, you'll end up with an HTML file that looks something like the left side of figure H1, and when you view it in a browser it will look something like the right side of Figure H1.

```
<HTML>
<H1>Marvin Somebody</H1>
<IMG SRC="me.jpg">
<P>Welcome to my home page.
I hope you enjoy your visit.
</P>
</HTML>
```

Marvin Somebody

Welcome to my home page. I hope you enjoy your visit.

FIGURE H1   HTML file on the left with a sample preview on the right. The actual appearance in the Web browser will depend on the settings used.

You can use the **WIDTH** and **HEIGHT** attributes of an **IMG** tag to change the size of a picture on the screen, but beware: a perfectly fine picture can end up looking awful if you aren't careful. Setting the **WIDTH** and **HEIGHT** to larger values than the original will show all of the pixels in the picture as squares, making it look like a tile mosaic instead of the picture you want. Changing the proportion of **WIDTH** to **HEIGHT** will make the picture look scrunched.

If you set the **WIDTH** and **HEIGHT** to values smaller than the original, the picture will probably look fine, but there is another problem with shrinking the picture. If the original large picture is 400K, then the file has much more information than what is needed for a picture that is 1 inch by 1 inch on the screen, so the time it takes to download the 400K file will be mostly wasted. This might not be a problem for one picture, but it could be a big problem for a set of pictures. A better idea is to reduce the picture before putting it on your Web site. Then viewers will only have to download what they will actually see.

In our Web site example, the home page will have a link to a photo album page that has several pictures on it. Let's make a photo page now, using what we know about how to put images on Web pages. You'll need to make a new file, since each Web page goes in its own HTML file. Call the new file **album.html**. You can use the H1 tag to put a heading at the top of the page, just as you did on your home page. Select a few photos (scanned in, or taken with a digital camera) to put on your page. If you don't have photos handy, you can use any JPEG, PNG, or GIF picture files for practice.

Use an image tag for each photo, and use the paragraph tag to put a caption below each picture. Here's an example:

```
<HTML>
<H1>Marvin's Photo Album</H1>
<P><IMG SRC="sunset.jpg"></P>
<P>Sunset in Hawaii.</P>
<P><IMG SRC="mountain.jpg"></P>
<P>My trip to the Rockies.</P>
</HTML>
```

Marvin's Photo Album

Sunset in Hawaii.

My trip to the Rockies.

FIGURE H2   A first cut at a photo album page.

Links

Now that you have two files, you'll want to link them together. This will let visitors to your Web site go easily from your home page to your photo album without typing in another URL. In this case, the tag to use looks like this:

```
<A HREF="photo.html">My Photo Album</A>
```

The tag for a link is an **A** tag with an **HREF** attribute. The value for the **HREF** attribute is the URL for the page to which the browser will go when the user clicks on the link. In this case it is simply the name of a file in the same directory as the home page (index.html). In other cases it can be the URL for a completely different Web site. For instance, a link to Sun's Java page would look like this:

```
<A HREF="http://java.sun.com">Sun's Java Page</A>
```

Note that in this case the URL includes the protocol, which is http (HyperText Transfer Protocol), followed by a colon and two slashes, and then the name of a Web server (java.sun.com). Since this URL does not include a file name, the browser receives a file with a default name, like **index.html**.

The text between the **<A HREF[[NotUpdated]]>** and the **</A>** tag is the link that the user can click on to go to the page. By default, links appear as underlined blue text. The default can be changed, either in the Web page or in browser options. In most browsers the cursor will change shape when it is over a link. In Netscape Navigator, for instance, the cursor changes from an arrow to a hand with a pointing finger when it is over a link.

When you add the photo album link to your home page, the HTML text will look something like the left side of Figure H3, while the page in the browser will look like the right side of Figure H3.

```
<HTML>
<H1>Marvin Somebody</H1>
<IMG SRC="me.jpg">
<P>Welcome to my home page.
I hope you enjoy your visit.
</P>
<P><A HREF="photo.html">My Photo
Album</A></P>
</HTML>
```

Marvin Somebody

Welcome to my home page. I hope you enjoy your visit.

My Photo Album

FIGURE H3   The home page example with a link to the photo album added.

Text is not the only thing that can appear between an opening **<A HREF...>** tag and the closing **</A>** tag. You can also use an image as the link. Generally a picture used as a link will have a blue rectangle drawn around it to show that it is a link.

If you want to link to a particular place in a document, you can use the **A** tag with a **NAME** attribute to define an anchor. If you wanted viewers to be able to go to the part of the photo album page that showed a trip to the Rocky Mountains, you could use an **A** tag like this one:

```
<A NAME="Rockies"></A>
```

Then, when you make a link to the page, use the # sign between the name of the page and the name of the anchor, like this:

```
<A HREF="photo.html#Rockies">Pictures from my trip to the
Rocky Mountains</A>
```

You can make a link to an anchor from another page or on the same page. For long documents, it is often convenient to have an index at the top with links to main sections of the document.

Text Formatting

Now that we have the basic elements (text, pictures, and links) in our home page example, let's take a look at text formatting. We've already seen the **<H1>** tag, which is used for a first-level header. There are other header tags that correspond to other levels of outline headings: **<H2>** for a second-level header, **<H3>** for a third-level header, and so on.

Another formatting tag that we've already seen is the **<P>** tag for paragraphs. A similar tag is the **
** tag, which puts in a line break (BR stands for "break"), also called a newline. Use the break tag whenever you want to end a line or put blank lines in your page. For example, you might want to put a blank line just before the photo album link in the home page. You could do that by putting in the **
** tag just before the **<P>** tag for the album link. Note that unlike the other tags we've seen so far, there is no corresponding closing tag for the break tag.

Another formatting tag which has no closing tag is the **<HR>** tag. HR stands for "Horizontal Rule" and can be used to draw a line across the page in an HTML document. Try adding an **<HR>** tag to one of the pages you've been working on. By default, a shaded line is drawn that has a three-dimensional effect. If you don't like that style of line, you can include the attribute **NOSHADE**, and a solid line will be drawn. If you want a thicker line, you can include a **SIZE** attribute, like **SIZE=5**.

If you don't want the line to go all the way across the page, you can specify a width as a percentage of the page. For instance, the tag **<HR WIDTH=50%>** will draw a line half as wide as the page. The line will be centered on the page, unless you also include an ALIGN attribute, such as **<HR ALIGN=LEFT WIDTH=50%>**. A width can also be specified in pixels rather than as a percentage.

Include some breaks or lines in your home page if you'd like to. For purposes of simplicity, the home page examples shown here will not include any.

HTML also provides tags to change the style of text, including making text bold, italic, or underlined. To make text bold, use the **<B>** tag. All text between an opening **<B>** tag and the corresponding closing tag, **</B>**, will be bold. Likewise, use and **</I>** for italicized text, and and **</U>** for underlined text.

Titles are often centered on a page. If you'd like to center the title of your home page, put **<CENTER>** and **</CENTER>** tags around it. You might also want to center your picture. After the title and picture are centered, the HTML and home page preview look like Figure H4.

```
<HTML>
<CENTER><H1>Marvin Somebody</H1>
<IMG SRC="me.jpg">
</CENTER>
<P>Welcome to my home page.
I hope you enjoy your visit.
</P>
<P><A HREF="photo.html">My Photo
Album</A></P>
</HTML>
```

Marvin Somebody

Welcome to my home page. I hope you enjoy your visit.

My Photo Album

FIGURE H4   The home page example with the title and picture centered.

Left alignment is the default, and you can use the **CENTER** tag to center text, but what happens if you want text to be aligned on the right? You can specify right alignment (or left or center) of text, pictures, or other page elements using the **ALIGN** attribute of the **DIV** tag:

<DIV ALIGN=RIGHT>right-aligned text</DIV>

For long quotations, you can enclose text (and other elements) in **<BLOCKQUOTE>** and **</BLOCKQUOTE>** tags. Text marked as **BLOCKQUOTE** is usually indented. Some browsers indent on both the left and right sides.

If you'd like text to be superscript or subscript, you can use `<SUP>` and `<SUB>` tags, respectively:

```
x<SUP>2</SUP> would be one way to write x squared in HTML
```

Page Properties

In addition to formatting text, you can also specify page properties in HTML, including a title and a background color. The title of an HTML page appears in the title bar of the browser window. To include a title in your page, you need to make a **HEAD** section for the document and then use the **TITLE** tag. For example, on the home page you might include the following HTML code:

```
<HEAD>
<TITLE>Marvin Somebody's Home Page</TITLE>
</HEAD>
```

There is also a **BODY**, to go along with the **HEAD** section of a document. The **BODY** tag can include attributes that specify the background color of the page and the colors of various kinds of text. Regular text, links, and visited links can each be given a color with the attributes **TEXT**, **LINK**, and **VLINK**, respectively. Colors can be specified by using names of colors, including **BLUE**, **RED**, **YELLOW**, **ORANGE**, **GREEN**, **BROWN**, **PINK**, **PURPLE**, **BLACK**, and **WHITE**. To specify that the page should have blue normal text, red links, with a background color of yellow, you could include the following tags in the page:

```
<BODY TEXT=BLUE LINK=RED BGCOLOR=YELLOW>
... All body text for the document goes here ...
</BODY>
```

Colors can also be specified by hex (base 16) values that have three components, one value for each of the red, green, and blue (RGB) components of the color. For example, instead of using the name **RED**, you could specify the color red as "**#FF0000**". The first two hex digits, FF, indicate that the color includes the maximum amount of red, while the last two pairs of hex digits, both 00, indicate that the color includes the minimum amounts of green and blue. A light orange or gold color can be made with the hex value **#FFCC33**.

In the **BODY** tag you can also specify a background image for a page. The attribute to use for a background image is **BACKGROUND**. The value of the attribute can be the URL of any image, but it is usually the name of an image in the same directory.

Fonts

Any text in an HTML document can be enclosed in **FONT** tags to change its characteristics, including color. For instance, the following HTML would show the word "Hawaii" in green. Note the closing `</FONT>` tag.

```
<FONT COLOR=GREEN>Hawaii</FONT>
```

By using the **FACE** attribute of the **FONT** tag, you can specify a particular font, like Ariel or Helvetica. However, a browser can only display text in a given font if the font is installed on the computer where the browser is running. Unless you choose a very common font, like Helvetica, chances are it will not be installed on the system running the browser and therefore will not be used. Even a font that is commonly used is not guaranteed to be available, so using certain fonts is often not effective.

TABLES

Let's return to the photo album example and consider the possibilities for organizing an album that includes 15 to 20 photos. You don't want to put that many photos on one page unless they are quite small, but if you make them small enough to allow a reasonable download time, they will be too small to be effective.

You could divide the photos among five or six pages, but then the viewer will probably have to download all of the pictures even if only a few are of interest. Also, going back and forth between the pages can be slow (depending on how the browser's cache is set up).

Another possibility is to have an index page that shows smaller versions of the photos. Smaller pictures are often called "thumbnails" because of their size. Each thumbnail image can be a link to a larger version. Viewers can choose which larger pictures to download by looking at the thumbnails, and thus do not have to download photos they are not interested in seeing.

If you decide to use thumbnail images on the photo album page, a good organization for the page is to use a grid, where each cell in the grid contains a thumbnail and its caption. You will need to use an HTML table to set up a page of this kind.

A table is made up of cells organized into rows and columns. Each cell of a table can contain text paragraphs, images, links, and even another table. The basic tag for a table is simply the **<TABLE>** tag, which indicates the beginning of the table. A corresponding **</TABLE>** shows the end of the table. Each row in the table is enclosed in matching **<TR>** and **</TR>** tags between the **<TABLE>** and **</TABLE>** tags. Within a row, the contents of a cell are contained between **<TD>** and **</TD>** tags.

You can start the new photo album page by putting each picture in a table cell, and then add the links and the captions later. Save the page with the table and load it into the browser. If you type in the left part of Figure H5, you should see something that looks like the right side of the same figure. As always, the exact placement of things depends on the size of the browser window and the size of the pictures. Remember, you will want to use small images with this table. You can use graphics software to make a smaller version of each photo. In this example, the name of the small picture file will have "_s" right before the dot in the file name, so that we can distinguish between large and small versions of the same picture.

You can put other formatting commands in between the **<TD>** and **</TD>**, such as **<CENTER>** and **</CENTER> or <B>** and **</B>**. You can also put in text for captions. The HTML for one cell in the picture might look like this after a caption included:

```
<TD><IMG SRC=rabbit_s.jpg><BR>My rabbit</TD>
```

You can center both picture and caption in the cell using HTML like this:

```
<TD><CENTER><IMG SRC=rabbit_s.jpg><BR>
My rabbit</CENTER></TD>
```

```
<HTML>
<H1>Marvin's Photo Album</H1>
<TABLE>
<TR>
<TD><IMG SRC="sunset_s.jpg"></TD>
<TD><IMG SRC="mountain_s.jpg"></TD>
</TR>
<TR>
<TD><IMG SRC="rabbit_s.jpg"></TD>
<TD><IMG SRC="fish_s.jpg"></TD>
</TR>
</TABLE>
</HTML>
```

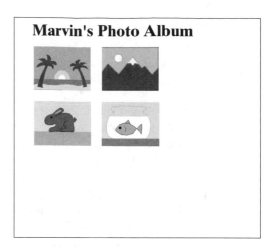

FIGURE H5   Using a table for the photo-album page.

Next you can make each small picture a link to the bigger version of the same picture. If you'd like to, you can make a separate page for each large picture. On the other hand, you might prefer to have the browser load just the picture. You can do this by adding a link to the picture file, which in this example would look the code shown below:

```
<TD><CENTER><A HREF=rabbit.jpg><IMG SRC=rabbit_s.jpg><BR>
My rabbit</A></CENTER></TD>
```

There are a couple of things to note about the preceding HTML code. First, with a link like this, the browser will load only the picture (in this case rabbit.jpg), and there will be no text or other information with the picture. If you want to include a caption, description, or links to other pictures, you will need to make an HTML page and have the link refer to the HTML file instead of referring directly to the picture file. The second thing is that both the picture and the text ("My rabbit") will be part of the link. The user can click on either one to have the browser load the picture.

There are many variations possible for tables. You can specify a background color or background image for a table, a row, or a cell using the **BGCOLOR** and **BACKGROUND** attributes, respectively. If you use an image for a table background, the results may be browser (or version) dependent. In Netscape Navigator, a table background image was repeated in each cell, whereas in Microsoft Internet Explorer the image was the background for the entire table.

The **WIDTH** attribute of a **TABLE** tag tells how wide the table should be, either as a percentage of the page width or as a fixed width. Similarly, each cell in the table can have a width attribute telling what percentage of the table it should occupy or how many pixels wide it should be. When specifying fixed widths, remember that the viewer's browser window may be larger or smaller than yours. If you make a table or cell too wide, it may not fit in the window and the viewer will have to scroll to see the entire table, which is inconvenient.

FRAMES

Suppose you want to include a navigation bar at the top of the page, and have it stay in view no matter how far down the user scrolls. You can do this by using frames. You can also make a navigation bar that is consistent from one page to the next.

The basic idea of frames is to divide the page into parts that can be scrolled and changed independently. Each frame has its own URL from which the content is loaded.

Use the **FRAMESET** tag to split a page into frames. The **<FRAMESET>** and matching **</FRAMESET>** enclose a set of **<FRAME>** tags, where each **<FRAME>** tag tells the source document for that frame.

Attributes of the **FRAMESET** tag tell the type and size of divisions. Each **FRAMESET** tag can have a **ROWS** attribute, a **COLS** attribute, or both. For each of these attributes, there is a list of sizes. The number of sizes tells how many rows or columns there will be. For example, in this **FRAMESET**:

```
<FRAMESET ROWS=10%, *, *>
```

will divide the page into three rows, where the first row takes 10 percent of the page height, and the remainder is evenly split between the last two rows. An asterisk indicates that the row takes an equal share of the remainder of the page height.

Row height can also be indicated in pixels. Specifying the height in pixels is useful if you have a graphical navigation bar that is a fixed height. In other cases, a fixed height is not a good idea because there is no way to tell how the viewer's browser is configured. If the viewer's browser window is too small, some rows won't be visible. On the other hand, if the viewer's font size is large, a fixed-size row might be too small to show more than a single line of text.

Specifying the size of columns works the same way. The width of a column can be given as a percentage of the page width, a number of pixels, or an equal share of the remaining width.

A **FRAMESET** tag can contain both row and column attributes. In that case, the page will be a grid.

The contents of the frames are given by **SRC** attributes in **<FRAME>** tags. You can also add a **NAME** attribute to a frame tag. Suppose you have put the HTML for the navigation bar in nav.html, and the photo album page is in the file photos.html. Then you could use a page like the one in Figure H6 to show the navigation bar in a short frame at the top and the photo album page in the main frame:

Let's take a look at the definition of nav.html. Your first thought might be to define it using HTML like this:

```
        <HTML>
<TABLE WIDTH=100%><TR>
<TD>
<A HREF="index.html">Home</A>
</TD><TD>
<A HREF="photo.html">Photos</A>
</TD><TD>
<A HREF="resume.html">Resume</A>
</TD>
</TR></TABLE>
        </HTML>
```

```
<HTML>
<FRAMESET ROWS="20%,*">
<FRAME SRC=nav.html NAME="nav">
<FRAME SRC=photos.html NAME="main">
</HTML>
```

FIGURE H6   A navigation bar in a frame.

However, if you define it this way, the new page will be loaded into the top frame when the viewer clicks on a link. What you want it to do is load the new page into the lower, larger frame. You can set that up by specifying a target for the links.

```
<HTML>
<TABLE WIDTH=100%><TR>
<TD>
<A HREF="index.html" TARGET="main">Home</A>
</TD><TD>
<A HREF="photo.html" TARGET="main">Photos</A>
</TD><TD>
<A HREF="resume.html" TARGET="main">Resume</A>
</TD></TR></TABLE>
</HTML>
```

Now the new page will load into the main frame when the user clicks on a link in the navigation bar.

Suppose that you next decide to add a link to Sun's Java Web site, at java.sun.com. If you add a link to the navigation bar, with a target like the others, then the Java Web site will show up in the main frame. If the user goes on to other Web sites from there, the navigation frame will still be stuck at the top of the Web page. A stuck frame annoys Web surfers. The way to avoid a stuck frame is to use the target **"_top"**. If a link specifies **"_top"** as a target, then the new page will open in the full browser window, instead of just a frame. The Java link could be added to the navigation frame like this:

```
<A HREF="http://java.sun.com" TARGET="_top">Java</A>
```

In addition to the **SRC** and **NAME** attributes, a **FRAME** tag can also include attributes that specify margins, scroll bars, and resizing. The **MARGINWIDTH** attribute tells how many pixels should be left as a margin on each side of the frame. Similarly, the **MARGIN-HEIGHT** attribute tells how many pixels to leave at the top and bottom.

If you don't want scrollbars on the frame, you can include the **SCROLLING** attribute with the value **NO**. You can specify that scrollbars should always be included with **SCROLLING=YES**, and to let the browser decide you can use **SCROLLING=AUTO**. If the **SCROLLING** value is **AUTO**, scrollbars will be included only if the document's size is bigger than the frame size. **AUTO** is the default value for **SCROLLING**.

By default, a user will be able to drag the line dividing two frames to resize the frames. If you want to prevent this, you can include the **NORESIZING** attribute in the **FRAME** tag.

Suppose you want to have a row of two smaller frames at the top of the browser window, with a single frame below it. You can't specify two rows and two columns, because you would end up with four frames. Instead, you can use a frameset to divide the window into two rows, one small and one large. In the first row of the frameset you can put a nested frameset that has four columns. You could set that up with the files doc1.html, doc2.html, and doc3.html, with HTML code like this:

```
<HTML>
<FRAMESET ROWS="*,*">
    <FRAMESET COLS="*,*">
    <FRAME SRC=doc1.html>
    <FRAME SRC=doc2.html>
    </FRAMESET>
<FRAME SRC=doc3.html>
</FRAMESET>
    </HTML>
```

BEYOND TEXT AND PICTURES

You can make great pages using the elements we've seen so far, but the possibilities of Web pages go far beyond text and pictures. Web pages can contain interactive elements in forms, programs in the form of applets, and multimedia elements. In addition, there are a multitude of plug-in components for Web browsers that allow virtually unlimited page content.

Applets

HTML pages can contain Java applets. The **APPLET** tag specifies the class to use for an applet and the size and width of the applet on the page. Here is an example of a basic **APPLET** tag:

```
<APPLET CODE=SpotlightApplet.class HEIGHT=400 WIDTH=300>
</APPLET>
```

The **CODE** attribute tells which class file contains an applet class—in this case, the **SpotlightApplet**.class. The **HEIGHT** and **WIDTH** attributes tell the dimensions of the applet on the page. You can use the **CODEBASE** attribute specify that the class files for the applet are in a particular directory.

If you would like to have two (or more) applets on the same HTML page communicate with each other, you should include the **NAME** attribute in the **APPLET** tag. In the Java code for the applet, use a call to the **getApplet** method in the **AppletContext** interface to get a reference to another applet on the same page with the specified name.

If you would like information passed from the HTML page to the applet, you can use **PARAM** tags, which go between the opening **APPLET** tag and the closing **</APPLET>** tag. For example, if you have an applet that animates text, you can pass in a text string as a parameter. Names of image or sound files are also common parameters for applets.

The following example illustrates the **NAME** attribute of an **APPLET** tag, the **CODEBASE** attribute, and the **PARAM** tag:

```
<APPLET CODE=CharDisplayApplet.class CODEBASE=Game
NAME=CharDisplay   HEIGHT=125 WIDTH=250>
<PARAM NAME="CharacterName" VALUE="George">
<PARAM NAME="BackgroundColor" VALUE="0x009900">
<PARAM NAME="TextColor" VALUE="0xFFFF99">
</APPLET>
```

In this case, the **CharDisplayApplet.class** file is found in the **Game** directory. The name of the applet is **CharDisplay**. There are three parameters to the applet, one for the character name, one for the background color, and a third for the text color. The values for the parameters can be retrieved inside the applet by using the **getParameter** method and passing in the name of the parameter as a string. The return value of the **getParameter** method is a **String**.

In earlier versions of HTML, the **APPLET** tag was the standard way to include an applet on a Web page. In later versions, however, the **APPLET** tag is deprecated and the **OBJECT** tag is the standard tag for applets.

Forms

HTML forms can contain various interactive elements, including buttons and text fields. This section will give you an idea of what you can do with forms, but does not attempt a complete description of form elements, CGI, JavaScript, and the other concepts involved in using forms.

Each form in an HTML page is enclosed in **<FORM>** and **</FORM>** tags, with **<INPUT>** tags nested inside the form. Form components include text fields, check boxes, radio buttons, and selection lists. Forms can also include buttons. There are two standard buttons, **SUBMIT** and **RESET**, and a third kind of button that has no predefined action. To include a form component, use the **INPUT** tag with a **TYPE** attribute that tells what kind of component it is, a **NAME** attribute to identify the component in information sent to the server (or elsewhere), and a **VALUE** attribute to tell what text will appear in the component. For example,

```
<INPUT TYPE="TEXT" NAME="text1" VALUE="abc">
```

specifies a text field named text1 that has the characters abc in it. As shown in this example, the **TYPE** of a text field is **TEXT**. Other **TYPE** values include **RADIO** for a radio button, **CHECKBOX** for a check box, **SUBMIT** for a submit button, **RESET** for a reset button, and **BUTTON** for a generic button.

Text areas (multiline text fields) and selection lists do not use the **INPUT** tag. Instead, text areas use matching **<TEXTAREA>** and **</TEXTAREA>** tags with text in between that will appear in the text area. The opening **TEXTAREA** tag can include **ROWS** and **COLS** attributes to specify the size of the text area. For example, you could include a text area like this:

```
<TEXTAREA NAME="textarea1">
This text goes in the text area.
So does this text, on the next line.
</TEXTAREA>
```

For a selection list, use matching **<SELECT>** and **</SELECT>** tags, with **OPTION** tags in between. Each OPTION tag identifies a choice for the user. Thus a user who clicks on the selection list sees a list of items to choose from. The OPTION tags all include VALUE attributes, and one can include the SELECTED attribute to make it the default selection. Note that the VALUE attribute does not appear in the component, in this case. Instead, the text that comes after each OPTION tag is what appears in the component.

Here is an example of a selection list:

```
<SELECT NAME="select1">
<OPTION VALUE="blue">sky
<OPTION VALUE="green" SELECTED>grass
<OPTION VALUE="yellow">sun
<OPTION VALUE="red">apple
</SELECT>
```

In this example, the user will see **grass** in the selection list when the form first appears on the page. A user who clicks on the selection list to see the choices will see **sky**, **grass**, **sun**, and **apple**. The **VALUE** attribute for the selected choice will be sent to the server as the value of the form element **select1**.

A **FORM** tag can include **NAME**, **METHOD**, and **ACTION** attributes. The **NAME** attribute can be used to refer to the form in other parts of the page. The **METHOD** can be **GET** or **POST**. The method determines how the receiving program or script will get the form information. The **ACTION** attribute specifies the URL of a CGI (Common Gateway Interface) program or script, or specifies **mailto** and an e-mail address to which the form information will be sent.

The following HTML code defines a form with four elements: a text area, a selection list, a text field, and a submit button:

```
<HTML>
<FORM NAME="test" METHOD="POST"
              ACTION="mailto:you@your.address.here">
<TEXTAREA NAME="textarea1">
This text goes in the text area.
So does this text, on the next line.
</TEXTAREA>
<BR>
<SELECT NAME="select1">
<OPTION VALUE="blue">sky
<OPTION VALUE="green" SELECTED>grass
<OPTION VALUE="yellow">sun
<OPTION VALUE="red">apple
```

```
</SELECT>
<INPUT TYPE="TEXT" NAME="text1" VALUE="" SIZE="50">
<INPUT TYPE="SUBMIT" NAME="sub1" VALUE="Submit">
</FORM>
</HTML>
```

If you use a form like the one defined above (with your real e-mail address), you will find that the e-mail sent to you is rather cryptic. Here is a sample response:

```
textarea1=You+could+write+an+essay+here%0D%0A
if+you+wanted+to.%0D%0A&select1=blue&
text1=I+chose+sky+in+the+selection+box.&sub1=Submit
```

Spaces have been replaced with plus signs, newlines appear as **%0D%0A,** and the end of a string is marked with an ampersand. You would probably want to write a program to reformat the messages.

Sending e-mail is one kind of action for a form, but it is not the most common one. Instead, the forms are usually used in conjunction with CGI. The basic idea of CGI is that you set up a program or script that will be executed on the server when the Web server receives a request for its URL. Not every ISP (Internet Service Provider) provides CGI capability, so you might not have that as an option. On the other hand, some ISPs provide standard CGI scripts that you can use on your Web pages. Some Internet sites provide free standard CGI service that you can use from Web pages on your own ISP's server. This works because the **ACTION** attribute includes a URL, so it can specify a server other than the server for the form's Web page.

When a form is used with a CGI program or script, the **GET** method will send the form information as the value of the CGI parameter **QUERY_STRING.** The **PUT** method will send the form information to the standard input of the CGI program or script.

Another way to make use of forms on a Web page, besides mailto and CGI, is to use JavaScript. You can include a button in a form that executes a script when the user clicks on it. The information from the form will not be sent to the server, but it can used to customize pages or to store information in the form of cookies.

Multimedia

The good news about multimedia on Web pages is that you can do it. Video and sound can be included in an HTML page and played by a Web browser. The not-so-good news is that what seems to be a simple thing can turn out to be much trickier than it first appeared. There are two problems. One is that the tags used for multimedia are either nonstandard or do not have standard implementations in the commonly used Web browsers. The other is that the success of multimedia Web pages depends on the configuration of the browser, and there are many different possible configurations.

Rather than trying to cover all of the possibilities, let's take a look at one example each of sampled audio, MIDI audio, and digital video.

Here's a sample tag used for sampled audio (a voice recording):

```
<EMBED SRC=file1.wav HEIGHT=60 WIDTH=145
AUTOSTART=FALSE SHOWCONTROLS=TRUE></EMBED>
```

This is an example of the **EMBED** tag, which is commonly used but is not standard HTML. This tag is supported by Netscape Navigator and is intended for use with various plug-ins available for that Web browser. At least some versions of Internet Explorer also support the **EMBED** tag. The example shown above worked with Netscape Navigator version 4.75 and Microsoft Internet Explorer versions 4.0 and 5.0.

Here's a similar tag:

```
<EMBED SRC=file2.midi HEIGHT=60 WIDTH=145
AUTOSTART=FALSE SHOWCONTROLS=TRUE></EMBED>
```

This tag was used for a MIDI file. MIDI is a musical notation designed for use with sythesizers. The advantage of MIDI is that the files are generally much smaller than a WAV (or other format of sampled sound) file. The disadvantage is that MIDI files can only be used for instrumental music, and not for voice recordings or sound effects. Also, a Web browser cannot play a MIDI file unless the browser is running on a computer equipped with a synthesizer. However, most commonly used sound cards (or integrated sound chips) include synthesizer capability.

An important thing to remember is that the suffix of the file name (in this case ".wav") can make a big difference in whether or not the sound will play correctly, since the suffix is one way that the browser determines how to play the sound. The preceding example worked better (in one browser) with the ".MIDI" suffix shown above than it did with the similar suffix ".MID."

Here's an example of an **EMBED** tag used for digital video:

```
<EMBED SRC=file2.midi HEIGHT=60 WIDTH=145
AUTOSTART=FALSE SHOWCONTROLS=FALSE></EMBED>
```

Note that in this case the **SHOWCONTROLS** attribute has the value **FALSE**. It was written this way because (at least one version of) Netscape Navigator never showed the controls, but Microsoft Internet Explorer would either show or not show the controls depending on the value of the attribute. In order to get a consistent Web page, the value was set to **FALSE**.

An important issue for digital video is the compression used to make the video file. There are various codecs (software for compressing and decompressing files) for video, and the video will not play unless the same codec used to make the file is also available on the computer running the Web browser. In light of this, you should make or use video files that use commonly available compression schemes. Even if several files all end in the same suffix ".avi," they might each use a different compression.

The size of the file is another important issue for video. Only the smallest, shortest, and most compressed video files will be small enough to download over a phone modem in a reasonable amount of time. Choose video files carefully, and always give users information about file size so that they can avoid a long download unless the file is of particular interest. Although higher-bandwidth connections such as cable modems are becoming more common, download time is still important for files as large as most video files.

The OBJECT Tag

Since the **EMBED** tag is not standard HTML, you may be wondering whether there is a standard way to include multimedia components in a Web page. The answer is yes.

The **OBJECT** tag is the standard for sound and video, and is even the new standard for Java applets.

The **EMBED** example shown earlier can work as an **OBJECT** tag in Netscape (version 4.75) with little change:

```
<OBJECT DATA=file4.avi HEIGHT=120 WIDTH=160
        AUTOSTART=FALSE SHOWCONTROLS=FALSE></OBJECT>
```

Other than the change from **EMBED** to **OBJECT**, the only change is to use **DATA** instead of **SRC**.

Although the **OBJECT** tag is defined as part of the HTML standard, its attributes and parameters are left open because they are used by the program that displays the object. That program is usually a plug-in or control and may not be part of the browser. You'll usually want to keep **OBJECT** tags as general as possible, and test them with plug-ins and controls that are commonly installed in browsers.

Java Programming Glossary

An abundance of Java resources is available on the Internet and in various print publications. To make full use of these resources, however, you must be familiar with the terms used in Java programming. Here are some commonly used terms and their definitions.

.class file—the output of the Java compiler. A .class file contains the byte code for the class. In order for a class to be used in a program, its .class file must be accessible to the interpreter.

.java file—the input to the Java compiler. A .java file is usually typed by the programmer using a text editor or the editor of an integrated development environment (IDE).

abstract—a class that cannot be instantiated. An abstract class is used as a base to derive other classes using inheritance, but it cannot be instantiated itself. A class that does not fully implement an interface must be declared `abstract`.

abstraction—hiding unnecessary details. Well-designed Java programs and classes do not require the user to understand the details of how they work. Instead, the user only needs to understand the interface, which is usually much simpler and easier to understand.

accessor method—a method used only to access the value of an instance variable. Accessor methods are usually very simple and often have a name that starts with `set`, like `setColor`.

address—a number that can be used to access a specific location in a computer's memory.

algorithm—a step-by-step set of instructions for achieving a desired result. Algorithms are not always written in a programming language, and are often written in pseudocode or English (or, of course, your language of choice).

API—Application Programmer's Interface. An API tells what classes or functions are available for use in application programs. The Java API is a set of classes and interfaces which can be used in Java applications and applets. For each version of

Java, there is the general API and many additional APIs (or class libraries) available for special purposes.

applet—a Java program that is part of an HTML page. A Java applet in a page is executed by a Java interpreter that is either a plug-in or is part of the Web browser displaying the page. As a security measure to prevent the spread of viruses and other problems, Java applets have restrictions on the kinds of input and output they can do. Although applets usually include text elements, they do not have the kind of text-only interface that some applications use.

application—a Java program that is not part of an HTML page. Java applications are executed by an interpreter, and can have a text interface, a window interface, or some combination of them.

argument or **actual parameter**—a value specified in a method call that is the value of the corresponding parameter in the method definition. *Argument* is sometimes used as a synonym for *parameter*.

array—an object in Java that allows a group of values to be referenced by a single name and an number. An array is one way of organizing a list or table of values. Arrays are especially useful when a program must work with a large number of similar values and it is not practical to assign a variable name to each value.

assignment operator—used to change the value of a variable. The assignment operator is typed as an equal sign, but it is better to read it as "gets the new value of" or "gets" than as "equals." For example, the statement x = y + 1; would be read as "x gets y plus 1."

assignment statement—gives a new value to the variable on the left-hand side of the statement. A constant value or literal value cannot appear on the left-hand side of the assignment operator in an assignment statement.

autoboxing and auto-unboxing—automatic conversion between wrapper-class objects and primitive types. For example, if an `int` value is assigned to a variable of class `Integer`, an `Integer` object will automatically be created by the autoboxing mechanism. Likewise, with auto-unboxing an `Integer` object value assigned to an `int` variable will automatically be converted to an `int` value.

backslash—the escape character, \. A backslash preceding another character means that the following character does not have its usual meaning. The most common use of a backslash in Java is \n for a newline.

base type—the kind of elements that make up an array. If `a` is a reference to an array, then the type of `a[i]`, for instance, will be the base type of the array. If the base type of the array is `int`, then all of the elements in the array will be int and the type of `a[i]` will be `int`.

binary search—finding a particular item by comparing the search key (item to be found in the list) to a list value. If the list value does not match the search key, then either the first part of the list or the second part is recursively searched. Binary search is a very efficient search method, but it requires the list of values to be sorted so that it can tell whether the first part or the last part needs to be searched recursively.

bit—binary digit. A bit is the smallest unit of data used in programs. Each bit can have one of two different values, 1 or 0. Eight bits make up a byte of data.

body of a loop—the part of a loop that is repeated.

body of a method—the lines of Java code between the opening brace and closing brace of a method.

boolean—a built-in data type in Java that includes only two values: `true`, and `false`. The most common use of boolean values is in if statements and loops, but they are used in other ways as well.

boolean expression—an expression that has a value of `true` or `false`. Boolean expressions are used in if statements and loops.

bug—a mistake in a program that causes it to work incorrectly.

byte code—the format of files produced by the Java compiler and some other compilers. Byte code is not executed directly by the processor, but is translated by an interpreter on a statement-by-statement basis into instructions that can be executed by the processor.

byte—a unit of information. A byte is made up of eight bits. The size of a file is measured in bytes, usually as kilobytes (KB, about 1,000 bytes), megabytes (MB, about 1 million bytes), or gigabytes (GB, about 1 trillion bytes). The memory and disk capacity of a computer are also measured in bytes.

call-by-value—a way of passing parameters to a method where a copy of each argument becomes the value of the corresponding parameter.

calling object—Every method call (except calls to static methods) is associated with some object which is the calling object. A method call consists of a reference to the calling object, followed by a dot, followed by the method name and the parameter list in parentheses. For example, in the method call `student1.setName("Martha")`, the reference to the calling object is `student1`. If a method is calling another method in the same object, the calling object does not have to be specified.

case-sensitive—lower-case letters are considered to be different characters than upper-case letters. For example, the names "Enterprise" with a capital *E*, and "enterprise," with a small *e* are two different names.

catch—A keyword used to identify an exception handler in Java. Every `catch` clause includes an expression that tells what kind of exceptions it handles. If a matching exception occurs, the statements in the body of the `catch` clause are executed.

central processing unit or **CPU**—the part of the computer that executes instructions. A computer may have more than one processor, with some processors being used for special purposes, such as running the display. The main processor is called the CPU.

char—a built-in data type in Java that is used to represent character values. A variable of the char data type can have a letter, digit, or punctuation mark as its values. There are other possible values as well.

child class—a class that inherits from another class. Other terms for a child class are *derived class* or *subclass*.

chip—an integrated circuit. Chips are the basic hardware building blocks for making computer components. In personal computers, the processor is a single chip, and the computer's memory is made up of a number of memory chips.

class method—another name for a *static method*.

class type—a class name used as a data type. Variables that have a class type (for example, **String**) are used as references to objects.

class variable—another term for a *static variable*.

class—a definition for a specific kind of object. A class definition tells what instance variables and methods each object will have.

class path—a list of directories, .jar files, and .zip files that contain the classes available for use in a Java program. The class path is important in cases where the classes used by your program are in different directories. If the class path is not set correctly, you will probably get a message for NoClassDefFoundError (no class definition found). There are two different ways you can specify a class path. One way is to use the CLASSPATH environment variable. The other way is to use the **-classpath** option with the **javac** and **java** tools. The advantage of using the **-classpath** option is that it can be specified for each different program, whereas the CLASSPATH environment variable is shared by all Java tools.

client—a program that communicates with another program. The other program is usually called a "server," and often the communication goes across a network. A Web browser is one example of a client program, because it communicates with a Web server.

comments—part of a program file that the compiler ignores. Comments are added to programs to explain what the program is doing. In Java, comments are enclosed in /* and */, or are the remainder of a line after two slashes (//).

compiler—a program that translates the statements in a programming language into instructions that can be executed by the processor of a computer. The input to a compiler is called the source code or source file, and the output is called the object code or object file. Usually, the object file produced by a given compiler can only run on one kind of processor. In some cases, such as Java, the statements in the source code are translated into a format called byte code, which can be executed on any processor for which an interpreter is available.

compile—use a compiler to make a **.class** file from a **.java** file. The Java compiler can execute a **.class** file, but not a **.java** file.

component inspector—a window that shows the properties of components and in some cases allows them to be changed. Some properties of components may not be changed.

component—part of a program. GUI components are sometimes called "visual components" because they appear on the screen.

compound statement—a sequence of statements enclosed in braces that is treated as a single statement. The body of a loop is often a compound statement. Compound statements are also used with if statements.

concatenation—putting two strings together to make one new string.

constant—a value in a program that does not change. In Java, a value can be named and declared to be a constant by including the modifier **final** in the declaration.

constructor—a special method that is called when a new object is created. A constructor always has the same name as the class. Constructors are often used to initialize instance variables of the new object.

controlling expression (of a switch statement)—the part of a switch statement that tells which case to jump to. In a switch statement, flow of control jumps from the switch statement to the case that matches the controlling expression of the switch statement. The controlling expression must evaluate to an `int` or a `char` value.

CPU—Central Processing Unit.

data hiding—another term for *encapsulation* or *information hiding*.

data type—an indication of the legal values for a variable or constant. Compilers use data types of variables, parameters, and constants to check for errors in programs. In Java, every data type is either a primitive type or a reference type.

data—information. Data can be text or numbers. It can be a single piece of information or a structure that includes many smaller pieces of information.

debugger—a program designed to assist in the process of debugging. Debuggers usually include a facility for following the execution of a program one instruction at a time (called "single stepping" through the program) and for displaying the values of variables in a program.

debugging—the process of finding bugs (or errors) in a program and fixing them.

declaration—part of a program that tells the name and data type of a variable.

decrement—subtract 1 from a value.

default case—the case in a switch statement that will be executed if no other case in the switch matches the value of the controlling expression.

default constructor—a constructor that has no parameters.

directory—a special type of file that contains information about other files. Directories are used to organize the files on a disk. Each file is part of some directory.

dot—an operator used to access a method, instance variable, or constant of a class. The dot operator is typed using the period key on the keyboard.

double—a built-in, floating-point data type. A variable of this type can have a wider range of values than any other numeric type in Java. However, arithmetic with double values (and other floating-point values) is not exact.

double equal sign—the equality operator, which is written as two equal signs with no spaces or other characters between. The equality operator has two equal signs to distinguish it from the assignment operator, which is typed as one equal sign.

do-while loop—a loop that has the test (or condition) after the body of the loop instead of before.

driver program—a simple program whose only purpose is to test a class or method. Often a driver will contain only test data, a method call, and a print statement to show the result of the method call. Using driver programs and stubs, a programmer can test parts of the program before the whole program has been written.

element—a variable that is part of an array.

encapsulation—a program design technique where details of a class's data representation are available only inside that class. One advantage of data hiding is that users of the class do not have to understand the details of the data representation. Another advantage is that outside code will not depend on the particular representation that is used, so the representation can be changed more easily.

environment variable—a variable maintained by system software that tells how a user's account is configured. Environment variables are used in different ways on different operating systems, so you should refer to the documentation for your operating system for more information.

escape characters or **escape sequence**—character sequence that has a backslash followed by another character. The backslash indicates that the next character does not have its usual meaning.

exception—an unusual occurrence. A programmer can anticipate exceptions in Java and designate some code as an exception handler to deal with the exceptional situation if it arises. Java includes an `Exception` class that is used as part of the exception-handling facilities available in the language.

extends—the keyword that indicates inheritance. In a class declaration, the name of the class can be followed by the word `extends` and then the name of one class from which the defined class will inherit.

field—a variable or constant in a class.

File Transfer Protocol (FTP)—a specification that tells how a file can be transferred across the Internet. An FTP program (called an FTP client) can be used to retrieve programs from a remote computer.

file—named set of data stored on a disk. Files used with Java programs include source files, class files, and data files.

final—the keyword used to indicate that a named value is a constant rather than a variable.

float—a built-in class used to represent floating-point numbers. The range of values for a `float` variable is much smaller than the range of variables that a `double` variable can have.

floating-point number—a number that includes a fractional part. Java includes two floating-point types, `float` and `double`.

flow of control—the sequence in which statements in a program are executed.

folder—another term for *directory*.

for loop—a loop where the initialization, test (or condition), and update expression all appear in parentheses after the word `for`.

form editor—part of an IDE that can be used to create a form using a GUI rather than using the programming language directly. A form editor allows components like buttons and text areas to be added to the form.

form—a component that serves as the base for a GUI in a program. The term "form" can also be used for part of a Web page that allows the user to type in information that will used by a program.

formal parameter—a parameter in a method definition. When the method is called, a formal parameter gets its value from the corresponding argument (or actual parameter) in the method call.

Graphic User Interface (GUI)—a means for a user to interact with a computer, where the user can use elements such as windows, menus, and buttons rather than type commands as lines of text. GUI is usually pronounced "gooey" rather than "G-U-I."

generic type—a way of leaving the element type of a collection unspecified so that different collection objects can have different element types. For example, one **ArrayList** object might have elements of **String** type, while another object of the same class might have elements of **Integer** type. The element type is specified using a type parameter, which is in angle brackets following the class name. Generic types can be used with classes that are not collections, but the Java collection framework is one place where generic types are heavily used. The generic type mechanism was added to version 1.5 of Java.

hardware—a physical component of a computer.

heading—the first part of a method definition, which tells the return type, name, parameter types, and parameter names. The method heading is often written on a single line.

high-level language—a language designed to be easier to write and read than machine language or assembly language. A programmer using a high-level language does not have to pay attention to as many details as a programmer using a low-level language.

HTML—HyperText Markup Language. HTML is the language used to define pages that can be displayed by a Web browser. HTML pages can contain Java applets.

I/O—input/output. I/O includes displaying things on the screen (output), reading information from the keyboard (input), getting information from the mouse (input), playing sounds on the speakers (output), and using the microphone to record sounds (input).

identifier—a name. In Java, variables, classes, methods, and interfaces all have names. It is important to choose meaningful names so that the program will be easier to understand. It is also important to know the rules for valid identifiers in Java so that you can avoid compiler errors and other problems.

implementation of a class—the way that a class does its job, including the way that it represents data and the statements its methods use. Other programmers who use the class should not have to understand the implementation to be able to use it.

implements—the keyword used to indicate that a class contains all of the methods required for an interface. A class can implement more than one interface.

import—tell the Java compiler that you are using a particular package. Your program will not compile if it uses a class from a package, and you don't import that package (or class).

increment—add 1 to a value.

indentation—the use of tabs or spaces in a program to indent program text from the left margin. Consistently using indentation to show which statements are controlled by the same loop or the same if statement makes the program easier to read and understand.

index out of bounds—an exception (runtime error) that occurs when an index value is bigger than the biggest valid index in the array. For instance, if an array has 10 elements, then the valid indexes will go from 0 to 9, so using the index 10 with the array would cause an index out of bounds exception.

index—an integer value used to specify an element of an array.

infinite loop—a loop that continues executing indefinitely. If a program is stuck in an infinite loop, you can often break out of it by typing CONTROL-C.

information hiding—another term for *encapsulation* or *data hiding*.

inheritance—a relationship between classes where the child class includes all the features (methods, variables, and constants) of the parent class. The child class usually also includes methods and variables not found in the parent class. Inheritance is important for reuse because it allows the parent class to be modified (by adding features to the child class) so that it can be used in more situations than if there were no way to easily modify it.

inner class—a class defined within another class.

instance variable—a data item that is part of an object. All objects in a class have the same instance variable, but each can have a different value for the same instance variable. Instance variables can be accessed by any method in the class. Although public instance variables can be accessed by any method in a program, instance variables are usually declared private so that there is less chance that they will be used incorrectly or receive an invalid value.

instance—an object of a class. All the instances of a given class have the same data items, but each has its own value for instance variables.

instantiate—create a new instance of a class.

instantiation—the process of making a new object of a class.

int—a built-in data type. Of the integer data types in Java, `int` is the one that is most used.

integer—a number that does not have a fractional part. There are four built-in integer data types in Java: `byte`, `short`, `int`, and `long`.

Integrated Development Environment (IDE)—An Integrated Development Environment is a single software package that includes various tools such as an editor, a compiler, and a debugger. An IDE is usually designed to work with a particular programming language, such as Java or C++, or sometimes with a family of programming languages like C, C++, and Pascal. Some IDEs come with a GUI (Graphical User Interface) editor to help programmers make software that uses GUI elements.

interface—A means for a person to interact with a computer, or a way for two computer components (hardware or software) to interact with each other. An interface that allows a person to interact with a computer is called a *user interface*.

interpreter—a program that translates source code or byte code statements into instructions that can be executed by the processor. Unlike a compiler, which translates an entire file, an interpreter translates on a statement-by-statement basis, where each statement is executed before the next is translated.

invocation—a use or call of a method.

iteration—repetition. This word can be used for the idea of repetition, or to refer to a specific execution of the statements in a loop.

Java Virtual Machine—a machine that can run byte-code programs. A JVM is a "virtual" machine because it is normally implemented in software as an interpreter, rather than built from chips and hardware components.

Java—an object-oriented programming language. Java is a relatively new language that is related to C and C++. Important features of Java include portability, simplicity, and easily used graphics and network communication. Java can also be used to write applets that appear on Web pages.

javac—the command used to run the Java compiler from a command prompt.

keyword—a word that has a special meaning in the Java language and so cannot be used as the name of a variable or method. **if** is an example of a keyword in Java.

linking—putting two or more object files together into one program so that methods in one call methods in the others.

literal—a value used directly in a program, rather than being declared as a named variable or constant. A literal can also be thought of as a value whose meaning is the same as its name. Examples of literals in Java include **42**, which is an integer literal, **3.14** which is a floating-point literal, **'a'** which is a character literal, **true**, which is a boolean literal, and **"hello"**, which is a string literal.

local variable—a variable that can only be accessed by statements in the method where it is defined.

logic error—an error with no compiler errors that terminates normally but does not produce correct results. Careful testing is important for avoiding logic errors because the compiler and interpreter cannot detect them.

long—a built-in data type for integers. The **long** data type can hold the largest range of values of all the integer types in Java.

loop—a sequence of repeatedly executed statements in a program. In Java, **for** statements and **while** statements can be used to create loops in programs.

low-level language—a programming language that requires the programmer to pay attention to many details. Assembly language and machine language are the two main kinds of low-level languages.

machine language—the lowest level of computer language. Each instruction in a machine language program can be executed directly by the processor. Different kinds of processors have different kinds of machine language, so a machine language program from one processor cannot be executed on a different kind of processor. A compiler translates high-level-language programs into machine language so that they can be executed.

main memory—the place where programs and data are stored for fast access by the CPU. Retrieving data from main memory is faster than retrieving it from disk, but most computers have much more disk space than memory space, so most data must be kept on disk. Also, main memory is volatile, which means that it loses its contents when the power is turned off.

member—a data item or method of a class.

memory address—a number that tells where in main memory a data item is stored.

method call—the place in a program where a method is executed. A program contains one definition of a given method, but can include many calls to that method. A method call to another method in the same object includes the name of the method and values for each of the method's parameters. A method call to a method in another object includes a reference to the object that contains the method, the method name, and values for the parameters.

method—an action that an object can perform. Many methods have parameters to receive information, and return values, to give information back. A method definition includes the method's return value type, the name of the method, the types and names of the method's parameters, and the statements that are executed when the method is called in the program.

mod or **modulus**—an arithmetic operator whose value is the remainder when the first operand is divided by the second operand. The mod operator is typed with the % key. For example, the value of `11 % 3` is `2`.

multidimensional array—an array that has more than one dimension. A table or grid has two dimensions and is one kind of multidimensional array. Three-dimensional arrays are also possible, but are not as common as two- or one-dimensional arrays. The number of dimensions is not limited in Java, but arrays with more than three dimensions are rare.

mutator method—a method whose purpose is to change the value of an instance variable. A mutator method should always check its parameters to make sure that the new value of the instance variable will be valid. The name of a mutator method usually begins with `set`.

named constant—an alternative to using literal values in code. A literal, such as the integer `60`, tells only its value and nothing about how it is used in the program. In contrast, a named constant, like `MAX_SPEED_MPH`, gives information about how the value is used (in this case, as representing a maximum speed in miles per hour). By convention, the letters in the names of constants are all upper case.

null—the value of a reference that does not refer to anything. Trying to use a null reference to call a method or access an instance variable will cause an exception (`NullPointerException`).

object code or **object file**—the product of a compiler. In the case of Java, the object code is called byte code, which is executed by an interpreter. In the case of some other languages, such as C and C++, the object code is the machine language of a specific kind of processor.

object-oriented programming or **OOP**—a style of programming that makes use of classes, inheritance, and polymorphism to improve the software development process. In particular, OOP is used to improve program organization and make programs easier to understand.

object—part of a program that includes data (information) and methods (actions). Objects in a program are used as models. For instance, one kind of object might be used to model bank accounts. Each account object would include data, such as the name of the account holder and the current balance, and actions, such as deposit or withdraw.

operating system—software that manages the resources (like memory and processor time) available on a computer and provides services (such as input and output) to programs.

output—information that a program produces or displays. The output of a program is usually displayed on a screen or written to a file, but it can also be information sent over a network or sound played on speakers.

overloading—making more than one method or constructor with the same name. When the compiler translates a method call to an overloaded method, it looks at the number and type of parameters to see which method to use.

override—when a method in a child class has the same name as a method in its parent class. Method calls will use the method in the child class, not the overridden method in the parent class.

package—a group of related classes. The Java API includes many packages that can save programming time and improve program quality by allowing programmers to reuse classes.

parameter—a value passed to a method. In many respects, parameters are similar to local variables. However, a parameter's value is given in a method call, whereas a local variable's value is not.

parent class—a class whose features are inherited by at least one child class. Other terms that are sometimes used for parent classes are *base class* and *superclass*.

polymorphism—a characteristic of Object-Oriented Programming (OOP). Polymorphism is important when a method call includes a reference to a parent class. The base-type reference could refer to any number of child-class objects, each with a different implementation of the method. With polymorphism, the method to call is determined at runtime and depends on the class of the object, not just the class of the reference.

postcondition—a result of a method. Part of documenting a method is recording the preconditions and postconditions of the method.

precedence—a set of rules that tell which operators will be evaluated first. In Java, as in algebra, subexpressions that use the multiplication operator will be evaluated before subexpressions that use the addition operator. For example, the value of 1 + 3 * 2 is 7, not 8.

precondition—a requirement of a method call that must be satisfied for the method to work correctly. For example, a method might have the precondition that a parameter has a non-negative value. Part of documenting a method consists of recording its preconditions and postconditions.

primitive type—a built-in type that is not a class. In Java, the primitive types are `byte`, `short`, `int`, `long`, `float`, `double`, `char`, and `boolean`.

private—indicates that a method or instance variable is accessible only from methods in the same class.

processor—a computer component that executes instructions. Many computers have a single main processor called the CPU, but some computers have two or more general-purpose processors that share the work load. Computers often have special-purpose processors, such as a graphics processor that produces the video display.

program—a sequence of instructions written in a specific language.

programmer—a person who creates software.

protected—indicates that a method or instance variable is accessible from methods in the same class, or from methods in a derived class, but not from any other class.

protocol—a specification of the way that two or more processes (or programs) will communicate. For two people to communicate, they must speak the same language and agree on whose turn it is to speak. Two programs that communicate have similar requirements, although of course the language they use is much simpler than the languages that people speak. Two commonly used protocols are HTTP (HyperText Transfer Protocol) and FTP (File Transfer Protocol). HTTP is the protocol used by Web servers and Web browsers to communicate. FTP is a protocol used to transfer files across a network from one computer to another.

pseudocode—a language used to write algorithms. Pseudocode is similar to code, and in some cases is written in a programming language. It is often a mixture of English (or some other natural language) and a programming language.

public—indicates that a method or instance variable is accessible from a method in any class.

ragged array—an array where each row has a different number of elements. A one-dimensional array would not be considered ragged because it does not have rows, but arrays with two or more dimensions can be ragged arrays in Java.

recursive method or **recursive function**—a function that calls itself. A recursive function must include one case where it does not call itself, or else it will continue indefinitely.

reference type—a data type that is a class rather than a primitive type.

reference—a kind of variable used with objects. In Java, every variable is either a primitive type or a reference. A reference can be used to call a method for an object or, in some cases, to access instance variables of the object.

reserved word—a word that has special meaning in a programming language and so cannot be used as the name of a programmer-defined method, variable, or class. Examples of reserved words in Java are `if`, `while`, and `public`.

return type or **type returned**—the data type in a method definition (before the method name) that tells what type of result the method returns. The return type void indicates that the method does not return a value.

return value or **value returned**—a value produced by a method. When a statement containing a method call is evaluated, the return value of the method is used as the value of the method call.

run command—a command that tells the Java interpreter to execute a program.

runtime error—an error that occurs while a program is running. In Java, runtime errors are usually indicated by exceptions.

selection sort—an algorithm for ordering a list of values. Selection sort operates by finding the minimum value in the list, moving it to the front of the list, and then sorting the remainder of the list in the same way.

self-documenting—code that is easy to understand without separate documentation. Using meaningful names (for variables, methods, and classes) is an important part of making code self-documenting.

sentinel value—a special value that shows the end of input. It is important to make sure that a sentinel cannot be mistaken for a normal input value.

sequential search—going through a list of values from first to last in order to find a particular item. Sequential search is the easiest search to program, but it is much less efficient than binary search.

server—a program that waits for a client to connect to it and request a service. Often the client connects over a network. A single server can normally handle requests from more than one client at a time. A server can also be a computer that runs server programs.

short—a built-in integer data type. A variable of type **short** has a wider range of possible values than a variable of type **byte**, but not as many as a variable of type **int**.

short-circuit evaluation—evaluation that stops when the value of the expression has been determined, even if not all of the expression has been evaluated. For example, in the boolean expression **(x && file1.isOpen())**, if the value of **x** is false, then the value of the expression is **false** and there is no need to call the **isOpen** method for **file1**. If the value of **x** is **true**, then the value of the entire expression is unknown until the **isOpen** method is called. For this expression, short-circuit evaluation will be used if **x** has the value **false**, but not if **x** has the value **true**. Java uses short-circuit evaluation, so if **isOpen** included a print statement and **x** were **false**, **isOpen** would not be called.

single quotes—apostrophes used to for literals of type **char**. For example, **'a'** represents the character value of lower-case letter A. Note that if the same letter appears in double quotes, **"a"**, it would be a **String** value, not a **char** value.

software—a program that can run on a computer.

source code or **source file**—a file that contains statements in a programming language such as Java. Source code is usually written by a person using a text editor, and is the input to a compiler or interpreter.

statement—code that performs some action or actions, like assigning a new value to a variable or calling a method. The body of a method in Java is made up of declarations for local variables and executable statements.

static—keyword used with a method or variable. See *static method* or *static variable*.

static method—a method that can be called using the name of a class instead of the name of a method. A static method cannot access any local variables defined for objects in the class, since the method call is not associated with any particular object. An example of a static method call is `Math.pow(x, 2)`, which would call the static method `pow` in the `Math` class. `pow` raises its first parameter to the power of the second parameter, so in this case the return value would be **x** squared.

static variable—a data item shared by all instances of a class. A static variable in a class can be accessed even when no objects of the class have been created.

string—text. A string contains some combination of letters, digits, and punctuation symbols. The term "string" is short for "character string." The Java API includes a class called String (spelled with a capital S) that provides a way of storing strings and methods for processing strings. String literals in Java are enclosed in double quotation marks.

stub—a very simple version of a method used for testing. The use of stubs allows you to test a method before the methods that it calls have been completed.

subclass—a class that inherits from another class. Other terms commonly used for the same concept are *child class* and *derived class*.

superclass—a class from which another class inherits. Other commonly used terms for the same idea are *parent class* and *base class*.

syntax error—an error that a compiler finds in a Java program. If a compiler prints a syntax error message, it means that the file does not contain a legal Java program. Even if the mistake is a minor one, such as a missing semicolon, the program will not compile and cannot be run.

this—a name that refers to the calling object of a method.

throw—cause an exception.

throws—keyword used to indicate that a method can cause an exception that it does not handle.

try—keyword indicating the start of a block which has exception handlers. The exception handlers follow the `try`-block and are declared using the keyword `catch`.

type—a range of values. Every variable or parameter in Java is associated with a data type that tells what values it can contain. Constant and literal values are also associated with a data type. The compiler uses data types to check programs and prevent some mistakes. Examples of types in Java are `String` (a reference type) and `int` (a primitive type).

type cast—a way of telling the compiler to treat a value as a different type than its originally declared type. For instance, suppose that total and count are both `int` variables, and you want to divide them to calculate the average. If you do not use a type cast, then the expression `total / count` will be evaluated with integer division and give an integer value as its result. If you use a type cast, like `total / (double) count`, then count will be treated as a double value and evaluation will use floating-point division and give a `double` result.

type parameter—a class name in angle brackets that tells what the element type of a collection class will be. For example, `ArrayList<String>` has a type parameter of `String`, meaning that the elements of the list will be `String` objects. Type parameters can be used with any class that uses a generic type.

Uniform Resource Locator (URL)—a Web address. A URL specifies how a resource (usually a file) can be accessed over the Internet. A URL includes a protocol (such as HTTP or FTP), a host computer, a path, and a file name for a file. For example, in the URL `http://java.sun.com/j2se/1.3/docs/index.html` the protocol is **http**, the host name is **java.sun.com**, the path is **/j2se/1.3/docs/**, and the file name is **index.html**.

uninitialized variable—a variable that has not been assigned a value before it is used. The Java compiler will produce an error message if a method tries to get the value of a variable before the variable has been assigned a value.

user interface (of a class)—the public methods (and public data items if any) of a class. In order to call a method in a class, a programmer must know the user interface, which includes the method name, the number and types of parameters, and the kind of value returned by the method.

variable—a data value in a program that can be accessed by name.

variable declaration—part of a program that tells the data type and name of a variable. A variable must be declared before it is used.

void—a return type indicating that a method does not return any value.

while loop—a loop that continues executing as long as its condition (or test) evaluates to `true`.

whitespace characters—space, newline, and tab.

window—a rectangular area of the screen that is associated with a particular program. Usually windows have a border of some kind and can be dragged from one part of the screen to another. The **Frame** class (in AWT) or **JFrame** class (in Swing) can be used to make a window for a Java program.

wrapper class—a class that is associated with a primitive type and provides methods for use with it. For instance, `Integer` is the wrapper class for the primitive type `int`, and it includes the method `parseInt` which can be used to convert the digits in a string to an `int` value. In some cases, such as storing an item in a `Vector`, a value must be an object and not a primitive type. In those cases, the value can be stored in an object of the wrapper class.

Error Messages with Explanations

Before you can use your Java program, you have to compile it. Before you compile it, you have to fix the compiler errors. Before you can fix compiler errors, you have to understand them. For experienced Java programmers, that is usually not a problem, but some error messages seem very cryptic to beginning Java programmers, and fixing the errors can be frustrating. The explanations in this section will help you understand what error the compiler is reporting. Once you understand an error, you are well on the way to fixing it and being able to use your new Java program.

USING COMPILER ERROR MESSAGES

Compiler error messages may seem like a nuisance, but their purpose is to help you write better programs. Every mistake that the compiler finds is one less mistake for you to find later, and it is much easier to find and fix a mistake when you know the location of the problem. The Java compiler finds many kinds of mistakes, but it does not find all of them, because to do so it would have to understand how the program is meant to be used, and that is beyond the compiler (or any other program). For instance, changing the lower-case m in **main** to a capital M does not cause a compiler message, but will prevent the program from working correctly (and will cause the **java.lang.NoSuchMethod** exception). Some errors (like a missing **main** function) will cause runtime error messages, and some errors, called logic errors, will not cause any error messages.

If you think you have fixed a compiler error, but still get the same error message when you compile, check to see if you saved the file before recompiling. Also, make sure that the file you're editing is the same file you're compiling. Sometimes there are two files with the same name in two different directories. If you change a file in one directory, but compile a file by the same name in another directory, the compiler messages will not go away.

When the Java compiler finds an error in your program, it will give a line number that tells where the error was noticed. Most of the time, the line number will be the line that actually has an error, but the mistake may be somewhere else in the file. Start by looking at the line indicated by the compiler. If that line looks all right, then read the message to see if you can tell which other part of the program might be the problem. For instance, if the message mentions a constructor of a class (see the example of an improper constructor definition below), check the definitions of the constructors. If all you have to go on is the line number given by the compiler, start at that line and work your way backward through the file, looking at each line in turn until you find the error.

Sometimes you get several compiler error messages for a program that looks reasonable. In that case, be sure to start with the first error message and correct it before looking at the later messages. This is because one error can confuse the compiler and make it think that perfectly good lines have errors. (Of course, compilers can't really think, and probably aren't really confused, but it's conventional for programmers to use these kinds of terms for compilers and other programs.)

When you find a compiler error message, take the time to understand the problem. If you make quick changes to your program just to get it to compile, you may be introducing problems that will be difficult to find and costly to fix later on. The explanations in the following sections will help you understand what compiler error messages mean.

MESSAGES WITH EXPLANATIONS

This is not a complete list of compiler error messages, but it will help you understand how to use some common error messages.

All of the error messages here, unless otherwise noted, are generated by the command

```
javac ErrTest.java
```

where **ErrTest.java** is a file that contains a program with one or more errors. In some cases, the complete error output is shown. In other cases, where some parts of the error output are not of particular interest, only the line containing the error message is shown.

```
ErrTest.java:3: ';' expected
        System.out.println("Widget Report")
                                              ^
1 error
```

This is an example of an error message that correctly describes the problem, a missing semicolon, and correctly indicates the location of the problem in the program. This type of error is easily fixed because it is accurately described and does not cause additional error messages.

```
ErrTest.java:8: '}' expected
    }
    ^
1 error
```

This is another missing punctuation error. The compiler expected to see a right brace, but didn't. When you fix this kind of error, be sure to find the right place to add the brace. Adding a right brace at the end of the file will probably make this error go away, but the end of the file may not be the correct place for the missing brace. Hastily adding a brace to get the program to compile might introduce a bug that is difficult to find later. Being consistent with indentation and where you put braces can help a lot in avoiding problems with misplaced braces.

```
ErrTest.java:10: 'class' or 'interface' expected
}
^
ErrTest.java:11: 'class' or 'interface' expected

^
2 errors
```

An extra right brace is usually the cause of this error message. Consistent use of braces and indentation helps prevent this problem. In some cases, an extra brace at the end of the file doesn't show on the screen because there are blank lines between the main part of the file and the end of the file. Another possible cause for this error message is a multiline comment that is not closed at the right place.

```
ErrTest.java:3: unclosed string literal
        System.out.println("Widget Report");
                  ^
ErrTest.java:4: ')' expected
        System.out.println("Wonder Widget Works, Inc.");
                                                       ^
2 errors
```

This is an example of cascading errors. There is really only a single error, the missing double quotation mark. However, the compiler prints another message about a missing parenthesis on the next line (line 4). Even though line 4 is fine, an error message is printed because the compiler considers the right parenthesis on line 3 to be part of the text that is in quotes. This example illustrates the importance of fixing compiler errors by starting with the first error message printed, because later messages may be cascaded errors caused by the same error that caused the first message.

```
ErrTest.java:2: cannot resolve symbol
symbol  : class string
location: class ErrTest
    public void main(string[] args) {
                     ^
1 error
```

In this program, the mistake is using a lower-case s instead of a capital S to declare the parameter to main. "String" with a capital S is the name of a class, but the compiler cannot determine what "string" with a lower-case s is supposed to be, so it prints an error message. Keep in mind that Java is a case-sensitive language.

```
ErrTest.java:3: cannot resolve symbol
symbol   : variable total
location: class ErrTest
          total = 0;
          ^

1 error
```

The "cannot resolve symbol" message can be caused by several different mistakes. In the preceding example, it was caused by a misspelling (specifically, using the wrong case for a letter in a name). Another cause of the message is when a variable has not been declared.

```
ErrTest.java:3: cannot resolve symbol
symbol   : class StringTokenizer
location: class ErrTest
          StringTokenizer parser;
          ^

1 error
```

A third cause of the "cannot resolve symbol" message, shown here, is when a class must be imported but has not been. For instance, a program cannot use the **StringTokenizer** class unless the package name (**java.util**) is given with it, or the package or class is imported. Here is the error message when a variable is declared as being class **StringTokenizer** without the package name or a proper import declaration.

```
ErrTest.java:6: cannot resolve symbol
symbol   : constructor ErrTest   (int)
location: class ErrTest
          ErrTest ref = new ErrTest(9);
                            ^

1 error
```

Yet another cause of the "cannot resolve symbol" message is a method intended to be used as a constructor but incorrectly declared. If you put a return type, even void, on a method definition, it will not be used as a constructor even if it has the same name as the class. If the compiler is looking for a constructor with one parameter, for example, and it doesn't find it because it doesn't recognize the method as a constructor, then it will generate an error message. This is an example where a mistake in one place, the constructor definition, can cause an error message in a completely different part of the program where the constructor is used.

```
ErrTest.java:5: possible loss of precision
found    : double
required: int
        i = x;
            ^
1 error
```

In this example, **x** is declared as a **double** and **i** is declared as an **int**. Because a **double** value has a fractional part and an **int** doesn't, copying a value from a **double** variable to an **int** will lose the fractional part. The error message calls this a "loss of precision." A similar error message results when a larger integer type is copied to a smaller integer type, like copying an **int** value to a **short** variable.

```
ErrTest.java:3: exit(int) in java.lang.System cannot be applied to ()
        System.exit();
                ^
1 error
```

The **System.exit** method takes one **int** parameter, which was left out in this case. This compiler error message is saying that a method with one **int** parameter cannot be used with a method call that has no arguments.

```
ErrTest.java:4: variable a might not have been initialized
        a[3] = 5;
        ^
```

In this case the Java compiler has prevented a null pointer exception. The code below shows an array reference declared, but no array has been created:

```
line 3:  int[] a;
line 4:  a[3] = 5;
```

One way to correct this problem is to use **new** to create an array. Obviously the compiler cannot prevent all null pointer exceptions, and in some cases it gives an error when a variable is initialized, but error messages of this kind prevent many problems.

```
ErrTest.java:4: int cannot be dereferenced
        something.print();
                 ^
```

The problem here is that the variable something has been declared as an **int**, but is being used as if it were a reference to an object.

```
ErrTest.java:1: ErrTest should be declared abstract; it
does not define run() in ErrTest
public class ErrTest implements Runnable {
       ^

1 error
```

This error message occurs when a class is declared as implementing an interface, but doesn't include all the necessary methods for it. In this case, the interface is **Runnable**, which requires one method, called **run**, to be defined in the class. Since **run** is not defined in this class, the interface has not been implemented and an error message is given.

A class does not have to include all the methods for an interface if it is abstract. An abstract class is one that cannot be instantiated, and is only used as a base from which other classes can inherit. The two choices in this case are to declare the class abstract, in which case no objects of the class can be created, or to include all the methods necessary for the interface. For beginning programmers, the most likely solution is to include all of the necessary methods.

This example refers to the **Runnable** interface. The most commonly used interfaces are the listener interfaces, such as **MouseListener**, **MouseMotionListener**, and **KeyListener**.

```
ErrTest.java:4: non-static variable x_coord cannot be
referenced from a static context
        x_coord = 3;
        ^

1 error
```

In this example, **x_coord** is an instance variable, and the assignment statement shown is in the **main** method, which is a static method. Calls to a static method are not associated with any object, so there are no instance variables accessible from static methods like **main**.

There are several possible ways to fix this error. One way would be to declare **x_coord** as a static variable, but that should not be done unless there should only be one value for **x_coord** that is shared by all objects of the class. Another way would be to use a reference to an object that has **x_coord** as an instance variable. A third way would be to move the statement to a nonstatic method. To choose the best solution in a case like this, you have to decide how the variable will be used and whether it should be an instance variable or a static variable.

```
ErrTest.java:5: array required, but int found
        a[2][1] =3;
           ^
1 error
```

In this program, the variable **a** was declared and initialized as a one-dimensional array, but accessed as a two-dimensional array.

```
ErrTest.java:5: incompatible types
found   : int
required: int[]
        int[] a = 3;
                  ^
1 error
```

This error message is caused by trying to assign an integer to an array variable. The Java compiler verifies that the types of values on both sides of the assignment operator are compatible. If the types on both sides are the same—for example, both are **int**—then they are compatible. If the type on the right-hand side of the assignment operator can be converted to the type on the left-hand side of the assignment operator, then they are still compatible. An example of compatible types would be assigning a **byte** value to an **int** variable.

```
ErrTest.java:8: unreported exception java.io.IOException;
must be caught or declared to be thrown
        line = reader.readLine();
                    ^
```

In this case, the **readLine** method is called in code that does not handle I/O exceptions (such as end-of-file or file not found). These exceptions cannot be ignored, so the method call must be enclosed in a try block with a catch that matches the I/O exceptions, or the method that includes the **readLine** method call must include **throws IOException** after the parameter list.

```
ErrTest.java:10: invalid method declaration; return type required
    public MyFrame () {
           ^
```

This error message could mean a missing return type as it says, but it could also mean that a method intended to be a constructor does not have the correct name.

```
Note: ErrTest.java uses unchecked or unsafe operations.
Note: Recompile with -Xlint:unchecked for details.
```

Unlike the other messages in this section, this message is a note rather than an error or a warning. One cause for this message is the use of a generic class, such as **Stack<E>**, with no type parameter.

When a type parameter is specified for a generic class, like **Stack<E>**, the compiler can verify that elements pushed onto the stack are the correct type. For instance, if a stack variable is declared as **Stack<String>**, the compiler can verify that only **String** objects (or instances of classes that inherit from **String**) are added to the stack. If no type parameter is specified, the compiler cannot check operations, and so this message is generated.

If no other type parameter is appropriate, you can specify **Object** as the type parameter. Then the note will no longer be generated, and the class can be used in a way similar to how it would have been used before generics were introduced in Java 1.5.

EXCEPTIONS AND RUNTIME ERROR MESSAGES

The Java compiler cannot find every error in a Java program, but some errors may be found by the Java interpreter when it executes the program. Of course, some errors cannot be detected by either the compiler or the interpreter, so you must be careful to check the results your program gives.

When a program crashes (stops running because of a problem), the Java interpreter will print a message about an exception or an error. **Exception** and **Error** are both child classes of the **Throwable** class. The difference between an error and an exception is this: Errors are too serious to handle, and the only option is to stop the program, whereas an exception can be handled, if the programmer included code to do so.

Some common runtime exception and error messages are listed below, along with a description of the probable causes of each message. All of the error messages here, unless otherwise noted, are generated by the command

```
java ErrTest
```

where the file **ErrTest.java** includes a **main** method and has been compiled to produce the **ErrTest.class** file.

```
Exception in thread "main" java.lang.NullPointerException
        at ErrTest.main(ErrTest.java:5)
```

The null pointer exception is one of the most common runtime errors. This exception occurs when a program attempts to access an instance variable or call a method for a reference that is null. In many cases the Java compiler prevents this exception by giving error messages for uninitialized variables, but it cannot prevent all occurrences.

```
C:\JavaDir>java ErrTest2
Exception in thread "main" java.lang.NoClassDefFoundError: ErrTest2
```

This message indicates that the class **ErrTest2** was missing and therefore the interpreter could not execute it. The problem has various causes, including spelling the class name wrong and entering the command in the wrong directory. Another cause could be that the **CLASSPATH** environment variable is set to the wrong directory. A constructor with an access specifier that is not **public** can give the same runtime error.

```
C:JavaDir>java ErrTest
Exception in thread "main"
java.lang.ArrayIndexOutOfBoundsException
at ErrTest.main(ErrTest.java:4)
```

When a program attempts to use an index for which there is no element in the array, an exception occurs. The code in **ErrTest.java** looks like this for this example:

```
line 3:  int[] a = new int[3];
line 4:  a[3] = 5;
```

The array created in line 3 contains three elements, with indexes from 0 to 2. The array has no element with index 3, so the exception occurs. Note that this is not an error that the compiler detects.

```
C:JavaDir>java ErrTest
Exception in thread "main" java.lang.NumberFormatException: A
        at java.lang.Integer.parseInt(Unknown Source)
        at java.lang.Integer.parseInt(Unknown Source)
        at ErrTest.main(ErrTest.java:4)
```

This exception was caused when the **Integer** method **parseInt** was given a parameter **"A"**. The parameter for **parseInt** should be a string that contains only digits (and possibly a minus sign as the first character), or otherwise the number cannot be parsed. Note that even whitespace characters can cause this exception.

```
C:\JavaDir>java ErrTest
Exception in thread "main" java.io.FileNotFoundException:
test2.txt (The system cannot find the file specified)
        at java.io.FileInputStream.open(Native Method)
        at java.io.FileInputStream.<init>(Unknown Source)
        at java.io.FileReader.<init>(Unknown Source)
        at ErrTest.main(ErrTest.java:6)
```

In this example, the program tried to open a file that did not exist. The programmer should check to see whether the file exists. If the file does exist, make sure that the name is spelled correctly inside the program. Also, check to make sure that the file is in the right directory.

```
C:JavaDir>java ErrTest
Exception in thread "main" java.lang.NoSuchMethodError
        at ErrTest.main(ErrTest.java:5)
```

If there is a call to method that is not defined in a class, this exception occurs. Ordinarily, if there is no method defined for a method call, the compiler will give an error message and will not compile the file. However, this exception can occur if a method is removed from a class, and that class (but no other class) is recompiled.

In this example, there were two classes, **ErrTest** and **ErrTest2**. **ErrTest2** contained a method called **missing**, and the **main** method in **ErrTest** contained a method call for **missing**. Both classes were compiled with no errors. Then the method **missing** was removed from **ErrTest2** and it was recompiled, but **ErrTest** was not recompiled. The main method in **ErrTest** still contained a call to the missing method, and when the **ErrTest** was executed, the **NoSuchMethodError** occurred.

This exception will occur if you try to execute a class that does not have a **main** method. If you get this exception when you have included a **main** method, make sure that the name is spelled correctly (all lower-case letters), and make sure that the method is **static** and takes one **String** array as its argument.

LOGIC ERRORS AND DEBUGGING

Sometimes your program will compile with no problem, and will run without any runtime error messages or exceptions, but will still not produce correct results. This kind of error is called a logic error, or more commonly, a "bug." The process of finding and removing bugs is called debugging and is an important skill for programmers.

The first step in debugging a program is to find the bugs. Unlike compiler errors and many runtime errors, logic errors can be subtle and difficult to find, so it is important to carefully test your programs. Choose a variety of input data that represents as many different cases as possible.

When a test case shows an error in the program, you need to find and remove the error. If it is not apparent which statements in the program are causing the problem, you can use debugging tools to find the difficulty. Sometimes, adding extra print statements is enough. Other times you will the difficulty want to use a tool designed specifically for debugging, like **jdb** (a debugging tool that comes with the Java SDK) or the debugging tools found in an Integrated Development Environment (IDE). These tools allow you to trace execution of the program and see when statements are executed, and also allow you to see the values of variables as the program executes.

Hierarchical Index

Classes in this index are listed in hierarchical format, with each child class indented one more tab than its parent class. Classes that are children of the same parent are in alphabetical order. Each entry in this index tells the name of the class, the page number of its description (if there is one), the package, and its ancestor classes. The ancestor classes are in brackets, with the parent being first in the list and **Object** last.

AbstractCollection, (no entry), java.util, [Object]
  AbstractList, (no entry), java.util,
    [AbstractCollection, Object]
  AbstractSequentialList, (no entry), java.util,
    [AbstractList, AbstractCollection, Object]
    LinkedList, 101, java.util,
      [AbstractSequentialList, AbstractList,
      AbstractCollection, Object]
  ArrayList, 92, java.util,
    [AbstractList, AbstractCollection, Object]
  Vector, 106, java.util,
    [AbstractList, AbstractCollection, Object]
    Stack, 104, java.util,
      [Vector, AbstractList, AbstractCollection, Object]
AbstractMap, (no entry), java.util, [Object]
  HashMap, 99, java.util, [AbstractMap, Object]
  HashSet, 99, java.util, [AbstractMap, Object]
Arrays, 93, java.util, [Object]
Boolean, 53, java.lang, [Object]
BorderLayout, 5, java.awt, [Object]
BoxLayout, 109, javax.swing, [Object]
ButtonGroup, 109, javax.swing, [Object]
Calendar, 84, java.util, [Object]
CardLayout, 7, java.awt, [Object]
Character, 54, java.lang, [Object]

CheckboxGroup, 8, java.awt, [Object]
Class, 55, java.lang, [Object]
Collections, 97, java.util, [Object]
Color, 9, java.awt, [Object]
Component, 9, java.awt, [Object]
  Button, 6, java.awt, [Component, Object]
  Checkbox, 7, java.awt, [Component, Object]
  Container, 12, java.awt, [Component, Object]
    Panel, 26, java.awt, [Container, Component, Object]
      Applet, 3, **java.awt**, [Panel, Container, Component, Object]
        JApplet, 110, javax.swing,
          [Applet, Panel, Container, Component, Object]
    ScrollPane, 31, java.awt, [Container, Component, Object]
    Window, 35, java.awt, [Container, Component, Object]
      Dialog, 12, java.awt,
        [Window, Container, Component, Object]
        FileDialog, 14, java.awt,
          [Dialog, Window, Container, Component, Object]
        JDialog, 114, javax.swing,
          [Dialog, Window, Container, Component, Object]
      Frame, 17, java.awt,
        [Window, Container, Component, Object]
        JFrame, 116, javax.swing,
          [Frame, Window, Container, Component, Object]
      JWindow, 131, javax.swing,
        [Window, Container, Component, Object]
    JComponent, 113, javax.swing,
      [Container, Component, Object]
    AbstractButton, (no entry), javax.swing,
      [JComponent, Container, Component, Object.]
      JButton, 111, javax.swing,
        [AbstractButton, JComponent,
        Container, Component, Object]
      JMenuItem, 120, javax.swing,
        [AbstractButton, JComponent,
        Container, Component, Object]
        JMenu, 118, javax.swing,
          [JMenuItem, AbstractButton, JComponent,
          Container, Component, Object]
      JToggleButton, 130, javax.swing,
        [AbstractButton, JComponent, Container,
        Component, Object]
        JCheckBox, 111, javax.swing,
          [JToggleButton, AbstractButton, JComponent,
          Container, Component, Object]
        JRadioButton, 125, javax.swing,
          [JToggleButton, AbstractButton, JComponent,
          Container, Component, Object]

Index